REACH OUT and TEACH

Meeting the Training Needs
of Parents of Visually
and Multiply Handicapped
Young Children

by Kay Alicyn Ferrell
National Consultant in Early Childhood,
American Foundation for the Blind

REACHBOOK

with contributions by

Sherrill Butterfield,
Boston College

Zofja Jastrzembska,
American Foundation for the Blind

Kristen Rapsher
New Jersey Commission for the Blind
and Visually Impaired

Consulting Editor: Judith A. Eisler
Photos: Janet Charles
Illustrations: Cynthia Stoddard
Design: John B. Waldvogel
Art Director: Stephen Fay

AMERICAN FOUNDATION FOR THE BLIND
NEW YORK

REACH OUT and TEACH

REACHBOOK text, photos and illustrations

copyright ©1985

2nd printing 1986   3rd printing 1992

by American Foundation for the Blind,
15 West 16th St., New York, NY 10011

REACH OUT AND TEACH
REACHBOOK ISBN 0-89128-128-2
PARENT HANDBOOK ISBN 0-89128-127-4

Printed in the United States of America

These materials were developed in part with Federal funds from the United States Department of Education, Special Education Programs, under Grant #G008103230 ("Meeting the Training Needs of Parents of Visually Handicapped/Multihandicapped Young Children"). However, the contents of this publication do not necessarily reflect the views or policies of the Department of Education, and no official endorsement by the Department of Education should be inferred.

Project Staff
for
Meeting the Training Needs of Parents of
Visually Handicapped/Multihandicapped Young Children

Susan Jay Spungin, Ed.D.
Project Director

Kay Alicyn Ferrell, Ph.D.
Materials Development Coordinator

Sherrill Butterfield, Ph.D.
Product Content Specialist

Richard E. Gibboney
Susan Islam
Media Specialists

Zofja Jastrzembska
Workshop Coordinator

Susan M. Kershman, Ph.D.
Evaluation Consultant

Kristen Rapsher, M.Ed.
Correspondent Teacher

Delma Ward
Wilbert Suber
Pam Smalls
Project Secretaries

Additional thanks to:

Nancy Akeson and Lois Harrell,
Variety Club Blind Babies Foundation,
San Francisco, California

Jay Boyle,
New Jersey Commission for the Blind,
Newark, New Jersey

Catherine Brooks,
American Foundation for the Blind,
New York

Mary Lynne Dolembo,
Children's Special Education Center,
Kansas City, Missouri

Harriet P. Foiles,
Delta Gamma Foundation for Visually
Impaired Children, St. Louis, Missouri

Lawrence Gardner,
Columbia University Teachers College
New York

Margaret L. King,
American Foundation for the Blind,
New York

Mary Anne Lang, The Lighthouse,
New York Association for the Blind

Robert Long, Ed.D.,
Connecticut Board of Education and
Services for the Blind,
Wethersfield, Connecticut

Ruth Migliorelli, Parent,
Pelham Manor, New York

Yonnine Mingus,
American Foundation for the Blind,
New York

Sheri Moore,
American Printing House for the Blind,
Louisville, Kentucky

Consuelo Mosquera, Parent,
New York, New York

Mary Ellen Mulholland,
American Foundation for the Blind,
New York

Linda Norris,
Massachusetts Commission for the Blind,
Boston, Massachusetts

Louise Reynolds,
Tennessee Services for the Blind,
Nashville, Tennessee

Rigden Family, Plano, Texas

Robin Roller,
Houston Lighthouse for the Blind,
Houston, Texas

Glen Slonneger,
Virginia Department for the Visually
Handicapped, Richmond, Virginia

Maureen Vinton, Parent,
Eastchester, New York

Introduction to the Reachbook

Reach Out and Teach consists of four parts: (1) a PARENT HANDBOOK containing information on early child development with activities and ideas you can use at home to help your child grow; (2) a REACHBOOK, or workbook, with sections to help you keep track of your child's growth and development; (3) a set of slide presentations, which are intended to give a quick introduction to the information in the PARENT HANDBOOK; and (4) a TEACHER'S MANUAL to help teachers adapt the materials for their own work.

The PARENT HANDBOOK and REACHBOOK are for your use, with or without the help of a teacher or counselor; they have been written so that you can use them by yourself.

The PARENT HANDBOOK and REACHBOOK refer back and forth to one another. They were written in such a way that you can read the HANDBOOK and then practice what you read by doing exercises in the REACHBOOK. Each time you finish reading a section in the HANDBOOK, a page reference, noted in an arrow, will direct you to relevant material in the REACHBOOK that will help you to see how you or your child is doing on that particular topic. As you finish a REACHBOOK section, another arrow will direct you back to the HANDBOOK to continue reading. Every time you read a new section, you will have a chance to apply what you have read *to your own child* or *to your own situation* before going on to a new section.

The first several pages in the REACHBOOK are similar to a baby book — records of height, weight, immunizations, doctor's reports, and so forth. If you are a parent of an infant, you can start right now to keep track of this information. If you are a parent of an older child, you may not want or be able to write in the information about your child's earlier years, but you can start to keep track from today on.

Because children grow and develop and change, the first time you assess your child you might find either that (1) she has learned some, but not all skills in that section; or (2) she has learned all the skills in that section. If #2 is the case — great; you can go on to another section. But if your child has learned only some of the skills, you will want to come back to each assessment from time to time and check on what your child has learned. This is called "reassessment" and is explained more fully on pages 18–19 of the HANDBOOK. The summary charts provided throughout the REACHBOOK will help you reassess because they help you see at a glance what your child is doing, and whether or not you've started to work on a particular skill yet.

Whenever you reassess and go back to an assessment page of your REACHBOOK, try to use a pen or pencil in a different color and always write the new date in at the top of the page. Based on your new assessment, update the summary chart in the REACHBOOK. Continue to do this as your child grows.

Start now to keep records in your REACHBOOK.

This REACHBOOK belongs to

_____

I was born on_____ , 19____ .

My parents' names are_____

and_____ . We live at

_____
(Street address)

_____
(City)   (State)   (Zip)

My parents started this book for me on_____ , 19____ .

PUT MY PICTURE
HERE

BIRTH INFORMATION

Place of birth: _____
(Hospital)

_____ , _____
(City)   (State)

Birth weight: _____ pounds, _____ ounces

Birth length: _____ inches

Who was there: _____

_____

Baby was:
- ☐ Happy
- ☐ Angry
- ☐ Screaming
- ☐ Sick
- ☐ Tired
- ☐ Difficult
- ☐ Sleepy
- ☐ Other: _____

_____

Mommy was:
- ☐ Happy
- ☐ Angry
- ☐ Screaming
- ☐ Thrilled
- ☐ Tired
- ☐ Upset
- ☐ Sleepy
- ☐ Other: _____

_____

Daddy was:
- ☐ Happy
- ☐ Tired
- ☐ Angry
- ☐ Screaming
- ☐ Sleepy
- ☐ Upset
- ☐ Thrilled
- ☐ Other: _____

_____

Sister was:
- ☐ Happy
- ☐ Tired
- ☐ Angry
- ☐ Jealous
- ☐ Sleepy
- ☐ Upset
- ☐ Thrilled
- ☐ At home
- ☐ Other: _____

_____

Brother was:
- ☐ Happy
- ☐ Tired
- ☐ Angry
- ☐ Jealous
- ☐ Sleepy
- ☐ Upset
- ☐ Thrilled
- ☐ At home
- ☐ Other: _____

_____

GROWTH RECORD

Age	Weight	Height
Birth		
1 month		
2 months		
3 months		
4 months		
5 months		
6 months		
7 months		
8 months		
9 months		
10 months		
11 months		
12 months		
18 months		
2 years		
2½ years		
3 years		
4 years		
5 years		
6 years		
7 years		
8 years		

RECORD OF IMMUNIZATIONS

Type	Date	Boosters
Tetanus	_____	_____
DPT	_____	_____
Polio	_____	_____
Measles	_____	_____
Whooping cough	_____	_____
Mumps	_____	_____
Others:		
_____	_____	_____
_____	_____	_____

HEALTH RECORD

Visual Impairment

Date you suspected a visual impairment: _____

Date diagnosed or confirmed: _____

By whom (doctor's name): _____

Description and cause: _____

_____

_____

Hearing Impairment

Date you suspected a hearing impairment: _____

Date diagnosed or confirmed: _____

By whom (doctor's name): _____

Description and cause: _____

_____

_____

Cerebral Palsy

Date you suspected cerebral palsy: _____

Date diagnosed or confirmed: _____

By whom (doctor's name): _____

Description and cause: _____

_____

_____

Heart Problem

Date you suspected a heart problem: _____

Date diagnosed or confirmed: _____

By whom (doctor's name): _____

Description and cause: _____

_____

_____

HEALTH RECORD

Breathing Problem

Date you suspected a breathing problem: _____

Date diagnosed or confirmed: _____

By whom (doctor's name):_____

Description and cause:_____

_____

_____

Mental Retardation

Date you suspected mental retardation: _____

Date diagnosed or confirmed: _____

By whom (doctor's name):_____

Description and cause:_____

_____

_____

Other Impairment

Date you suspected:_____

Date diagnosed or confirmed: _____

By whom (doctor's name):_____

Description and cause:_____

_____

_____

Other Impairment

Date you suspected:_____

Date diagnosed or confirmed: _____

By whom (doctor's name):_____

Description and cause:_____

_____

_____

Ask your doctor or hospital for a written report of your child's eye examination. Attach it here. Make sure you understand what the report says.

If you don't understand it, ask the doctor to explain the report to you. If you still do not understand what it means, read pages 43–69 in the PARENT HANDBOOK. Then take the REACHBOOK to your next doctor's appointment, and ask the doctor to answer your questions.

DENTAL RECORD

Central incisors

Lateral incisors

Cuspids

First molar

Second molar

Second molar

First molar

Cuspids

Lateral incisors

Central incisors

Upper	**Dates**		
Central incisor	(1)_____	(2)_____
Lateral incisor	(5)_____	(6)_____
Cuspid	(9)_____	(10)_____
First molar	(13)_____	(14)_____
Second molar	(17)_____	(18)_____

Lower	**Dates**		
Central incisor	(3)_____	(4)_____
Lateral incisor	(7)_____	(8)_____
Cuspid	(11)_____	(12)_____
First molar	(15)_____	(16)_____
Second molar	(19)_____	(20)_____

IMPORTANT PHONE NUMBERS TO REMEMBER

Pediatrician's name: _____

Phone: _____

Ophthalmologist's name: _____

Phone: _____

Optometrist's name: _____

Phone: _____

Audiologists's name: _____

Phone: _____

Neurologist's name: _____

Phone: _____

Dentist's name: _____

Phone: _____

Orthopedist's name: _____

Phone: _____

Occupational therapist's name: _____

Phone: _____

Physical therapist's name: _____

Phone: _____

Psychologist's name: _____

Phone: _____

Social worker's name: _____

Phone: _____

IMPORTANT PHONE NUMBERS TO REMEMBER

Teacher's name: _____

Phone: _____

Orientation & mobility
specialist's name:_____

Phone: _____

Babysitter's name:_____

Phone: _____

Others:

Name: _____

Phone: _____

Name: _____

Phone: _____

Name: _____

Phone: _____

Name: _____

Phone: _____

Name: _____

Phone: _____

RECORD OF DOCTORS' VISITS

Date: _____

Doctor's name: _____

Why visited: _____

What doctor said: _____

_____

Date: _____

Doctor's name: _____

Why visited: _____

What doctor said: _____

_____

Date: _____

Doctor's name: _____

Why visited: _____

What doctor said: _____

_____

Date: _____

Doctor's name: _____

Why visited: _____

What doctor said: _____

_____

Date: _____

Doctor's name: _____

Why visited: _____

What doctor said: _____

_____

Date: _____

Doctor's name: _____

Why visited: _____

What doctor said: _____

_____

RECORD OF DOCTORS' VISITS

Date: _____

Doctor's name: _____

Why visited: _____

What doctor said: _____

_____

Date: _____

Doctor's name: _____

Why visited: _____

What doctor said: _____

_____

Date: _____

Doctor's name: _____

Why visited: _____

What doctor said: _____

_____

Date: _____

Doctor's name: _____

Why visited: _____

What doctor said: _____

_____

Date: _____

Doctor's name: _____

Why visited: _____

What doctor said: _____

_____

Date: _____

Doctor's name: _____

Why visited: _____

What doctor said: _____

_____

RECORD OF HOSPITALIZATIONS

Date: _____

Name of hospital: _____

Reason for hospitalization: _____

What happened, and outcome: _____

_____

_____

_____

Date: _____

Name of hospital: _____

Reason for hospitalization: _____

What happened, and outcome: _____

_____

_____

_____

Date: _____

Name of hospital: _____

Reason for hospitalization: _____

What happened, and outcome: _____

_____

_____

_____

Date: _____

Name of hospital: _____

Reason for hospitalization: _____

What happened, and outcome: _____

_____

_____

_____

Date: _____

Name of hospital: _____

Reason for hospitalization: _____

What happened, and outcome: _____

_____

_____

RECORD OF HOSPITALIZATIONS

Date: _____

Name of hospital: _____

Reason for hospitalization: _____

What happened, and outcome: _____

_____

_____

_____

Date: _____

Name of hospital: _____

Reason for hospitalization: _____

What happened, and outcome: _____

_____

_____

_____

Date: _____

Name of hospital: _____

Reason for hospitalization: _____

What happened, and outcome: _____

_____

_____

_____

Date: _____

Name of hospital: _____

Reason for hospitalization: _____

What happened, and outcome: _____

_____

_____

_____

◀ Turn to page 7 in the HANDBOOK

GETTING STARTED:

Learning About Learning

Reading Your Child's Signals

Today's date _____
Your child's
age today _____

How do you know when your child is looking? (Check all that apply.)

☐ Holds head certain way   ☐ Eyes move around fast
☐ Puts hand in/over eye   ☐ One eye wanders
☐ Looks surprised   ☐ Eyes come close together
☐ Brings object up close to eyes   ☐ Seems to concentrate

☐ Other: _____

_____

How do you know when your child is listening? (Check all that apply.)

☐ Gets quiet   ☐ Breathing changes
☐ Gets still   ☐ Eyes move around fast

☐ Other: _____

_____

Does your baby smile when you talk to her?   ☐ Yes
     ☐ No

Do you sometimes feel that your child doesn't know you?   ☐ Yes
     ☐ No

How does that make you feel?

_____

_____

_____

What does your child do when you pick her up? (Check all that apply.)

☐ Gets stiff   ☐ Cries
☐ Blinks   ☐ Laughs
☐ Snuggles up   ☐ Looks surprised

☐ Other: _____

_____

Reading Your Child's Signals

What could you do to give your child signals about who you are?
(Check all that apply.)

☐ Talk to her   ☐ Stroke her arm or tummy
☐ Play a game   ☐ Tickle her under the chin
☐ Carry her with you and talk to her
   as you move around the house

Other ideas: _____

_____

_____

How many of these have your tried before?_____

Sometimes a child — any child — needs to hear or feel these things
over and over again before she catches on. Keep trying. Your child
does know you; she just has a different way of showing it. Give her
a chance to prove it.

Turn to page 10 in the HANDBOOK

Chapter 1. GETTING STARTED
Who is Really Doing the Teaching?

Today's date_____
Your child's
age today _____

If your child has a teacher, how much time did the teacher spend
with your child today?

☐ Less than 1 hour   ☐ 4-8 hours
☐ About an hour   ☐ 8-16 hours
☐ 2-4 hours   ☐ 16-24 hours
                            ☐ No lesson today

How much time was your child with you today?

☐ Less than 1 hour   ☐ 4-8 hours
☐ About an hour   ☐ 8-16 hours
☐ 2-4 hours   ☐ 16-24 hours
                            ☐ Did not see my child today

If your child has a teacher, where did the teacher spend time with
your child today? (Check all that apply.)

☐ Child's bedroom   ☐ Garage
☐ Your bedroom   ☐ Outdoors
☐ Living room   ☐ Grocery store
☐ Family room   ☐ School
☐ Dining room   ☐ Post office
☐ Kitchen   ☐ Car
☐ Bathroom   ☐ Shopping mall
☐ Hospital   ☐ Restaurant
☐ Therapy room   ☐ Bus or subway

Other:_____

Where were you when you and your child were together today?
(Check all that apply.)

☐ Child's bedroom   ☐ Garage
☐ Your bedroom   ☐ Outdoors
☐ Living room   ☐ Grocery store
☐ Family room   ☐ School
☐ Dining room   ☐ Post office
☐ Kitchen   ☐ Car
☐ Bathroom   ☐ Shopping mall
☐ Hospital   ☐ Restaurant
☐ Therapy room   ☐ Bus or subway

Other:_____

Has your child ever helped you do, or been with you when you've
done, any of the following chores? (Check all that apply.)

☐ Wash clothes   ☐ Take other children to school
☐ Go shopping   ☐ Sweep or vacuum
☐ Wash dishes   ☐ Make beds
☐ Cook meals   ☐ Scrub bathtub

Other:_____

What did your child play with at home today? (Check all that apply.)

☐ Toys the teacher left   ☐ Laundry
☐ Toys you purchased   ☐ Clothes in drawers
☐ Pots and pans   ☐ Swing or slide
☐ Plastic bowls   ☐ Sandbox
☐ Boxes of food   ☐ Dishes in sink
☐ Mobile   ☐ Fingers or hands
☐ Silverware   ☐ Wooden spoons

Other:_____

Who is Really Doing the Teaching?

In the last week, how many of these people has your child spent time with? (Check all that apply.)

☐ Mom   ☐ Aunt
☐ Dad   ☐ Uncle
☐ Sister   ☐ Cousin
☐ Brother   ☐ Adult neighbor
☐ Grandmother   ☐ Child neighbor
☐ Grandfather   ☐ Your best friend
☐ Baby-sitter   ☐ Your child's best friend
☐ Doctor   ☐ Physical or occupational
☐ Teacher   therapist

Other:_____

_____

Did your child do something recently that made you think, "Just like me" or "Just like his brother?" What was it?

_____

_____

_____

What does your child do today that he didn't do last month?

_____

_____

_____

What did your child learn in the past couple of months that you knew *you* and not his teacher had taught him?

_____

_____

_____

What would you like to teach your child to do next month?

_____

_____

◄ Turn to page 11 in the HANDBOOK

Chapter 1. GETTING STARTED
Using Natural Interaction Times

Today's date _____
Your child's
age today _____

On a normal day, how many times do you:

Help your child get dressed? _____
Help your child take a bath? _____
Eat meals with your child? _____
Change your child's diaper? _____
Help your child use the toilet? _____
Change your child's position? _____
Help your child wash his hands? _____

During those times, is your child generally:

☐ Happy   ☐ Curious
☐ Angry   ☐ Difficult
☐ Unhappy   ☐ Crying
☐ Talkative   ☐ Quiet
☐ Not paying attention ☐ Asking a lot of questions
☐ Tuning out   ☐ Giggling

Other:_____

How do *you* feel during those times?

☐ Happy   ☐ Sometimes good, sometimes bad
☐ Unhappy   ☐ Irritated
☐ Talkative   ☐ Tired
☐ Excited   ☐ Okay
☐ Bored   ☐ About average
☐ Tied down   ☐ Frustrated

Other:_____

What have you done or could you do when your child is getting
dressed? (Check all that apply.)

☐ Talk to him, explain what's going on
☐ Have him pull his pants up
☐ Have him put his socks on
☐ Ask him to feel his diaper and tell you whether it's wet or dry
☐ Show him how to put his arms in the sleeves
☐ Talk about how each piece of clothing feels
☐ Talk about which piece of clothing goes on which body part

☐ Other: _____

_____

Using Natural Interaction Times

Does your child eat meals with you and the rest of the family, or
do you feed him alone, at a different time?   ☐ With family
                                              ☐ Alone

Are those times:
    ☐ Happy
    ☐ Messy
    ☐ Funny
    ☐ Frustrating
    ☐ Loud, noisy

Why? _____

What foods do you think it might be interesting for your child to
touch, smell, eat, and learn from? (Check all that apply.)
    ☐ Jello   ☐ Oranges
    ☐ Pudding   ☐ Breads
    ☐ Cheese   ☐ Mashed potatoes
    ☐ Apples   ☐ Peas
    ☐ Eggs   ☐ Parsley

    Other:_____

Which of these foods has your child actually eaten?
    ☐ Jello   ☐ Oranges
    ☐ Pudding   ☐ Breads
    ☐ Cheese   ☐ Mashed potatoes
    ☐ Apples   ☐ Peas
    ☐ Eggs   ☐ Parsley

    Others:_____

Toys that are brightly colored and use two or more senses are
especially good for visually and multiply handicapped children.

    Check the colors which you think are most interesting for your child:
    ☐ Red   ☐ White
    ☐ Yellow   ☐ Green
    ☐ Orange   ☐ Pink
    ☐ Black   ☐ Grey
    What other colors   ☐ Hot pink
    does your child like? _____

Which of these toys or objects in the home would make children use two or more senses? (Check all that apply.)

- ☐ Food
- ☐ Drum
- ☐ Television
- ☐ Mirror
- ☐ Pots and pans
- ☐ Blankets

- ☐ Radio
- ☐ Busy box
- ☐ Plastic bowls
- ☐ Rattle
- ☐ Wooden spoons
- ☐ Magazines, catalogs

Can you think of a toy that:

Has both moving and noise-making parts?_____

Has both a touching and a smelling part? _____

Uses both vision and hearing? _____

Uses both vision and touching? _____

Uses vision, touching, hearing, and movement? _____

Uses vision, touching, hearing, and smelling?_____

List other toys or common household objects that would be good for your child to play with:

_____

_____

_____

_____

_____

From where you are sitting right now, how many different textures can you see in your home? Write them here:

_____

_____

_____

_____

_____

Turn to page 15 in the HANDBOOK →

Chapter 1. GETTING STARTED
Excuses and Expectations

Today's date _____
Your child's
age today _____

Many people say that blind, visually, and multiply handicapped
children cannot do the things listed below. What do you think?
Check the ones that *you* do not think visually or multiply
handicapped children can do:

- ☐ Sit
- ☐ Walk
- ☐ Feed self
- ☐ Talk
- ☐ Run
- ☐ Walk to school
- ☐ Cook dinner
- ☐ Choose own clothes
- ☐ Read print

- ☐ Jump
- ☐ Ride a bicycle
- ☐ Drive a car
- ☐ Play baseball, football, or other team sports
- ☐ Play a musical instrument
- ☐ Live in own apartment
- ☐ Use a computer
- ☐ Hold a job

Now go through this list again, but think only about *your* child.
Check those that you think she will do. For those things that you
do not think she will be able to do, write down why you think so.

My child will not be able to do this because:

- ☐ Sit _____
- ☐ Walk _____
- ☐ Feed self _____
- ☐ Talk _____
- ☐ Run _____
- ☐ Walk to school _____
- ☐ Cook dinner _____
- ☐ Choose own clothes _____
- ☐ Read print _____
- ☐ Jump _____
- ☐ Ride a bicycle _____
- ☐ Drive a car _____
- ☐ Play baseball, football, or

    other team sports _____
- ☐ Play a musical instrument _____
- ☐ Live in own apartment _____
- ☐ Use a computer _____
- ☐ Hold a job _____

Now, look at the reasons why you think your child will not be able to do some of these things. Try to separate out those that are based on fact (like, "she won't be able to drive a car because she's blind and can't see") from fiction (for example, "she won't be able to play football because she's a girl").

Maybe you have placed a limit on what your child can do because you don't know that many blind, visually handicapped, and multiply handicapped adults *can* and *do* do these things, or maybe someone else has told you that your child will never walk, or never be able to live away from home.

What do you *really* think?

Turn to page 16 in the HANDBOOK

Chapter 1. GETTING STARTED
How Teachers Teach

Today's date _____
Your child's
age today _____

Choose a time when your child is playing alone happily. Sit down with this REACHBOOK and watch very carefully for one minute.

Now, on the rest of this page, write down everything your child does in another one-minute period. Put in as much detail as you can — even write down the little things ("he blinked" or "she was looking at the toy real close and jumped when the phone rang").

_____

_____

_____

_____

_____

_____

_____

_____

_____

_____

_____

_____

Turn to page 16 in the HANDBOOK

Chapter 1. GETTING STARTED
How Teachers Teach, continued

Today's date _____
Your child's
age today _____

Here are some skills that a child needs in order to feed herself with a spoon.

Task analyze: Number each skill in the order in which it occurs.
Assess: Check those skills your child can do today.
Plan: Put a star (*) at the skill your child should learn next.

	Step Number	Child Does Now	Child Needs to Learn Next
Brings spoon and food to mouth	_____	_____	_____
Swallows food	_____	_____	_____
Chews food	_____	_____	_____
Takes food into mouth	_____	_____	_____
Grasps spoon in hand	_____	_____	_____
Scoops food with spoon	_____	_____	_____
Returns spoon to dish to scoop more food	_____	_____	_____

How did you do? The first column should be numbered, from top to bottom,

3
6
5
4
1
2
7

Now try this task analysis for walking:

	Step Number	Child Does Now	Child Needs to Learn Next
Walks sideways holding onto furniture	_____	_____	_____
Balances on one foot	_____	_____	_____
Lifts one foot	_____	_____	_____
Moves one foot forward	_____	_____	_____
Stands alone holding onto furniture	_____	_____	_____
Repeats with opposite foot	_____	_____	_____
Maintains balance with one foot in front of the other	_____	_____	_____

How Teachers Teach

This time, the "Step Number" column should read from top to bottom,

2

4

3

5

1

7

6

Think of something you want your child to learn. Do the activity
yourself. Now, use the space below to write down each critical step:

Steps

1. _____

2. _____

3. _____

4. _____

5. _____

6. _____

7. _____

8. _____

9. _____

10. _____

◄ Turn to page 17 in the HANDBOOK

Chapter 1. GETTING STARTED
How Teachers Teach, continued

Today's date _____
Your child's
age today _____

Here is a list of things adults say to children. Check off those that you think give children good verbal feedback:

- ☐ "Good. You stacked the blocks."
- ☐ "You did a nice job putting your puzzle together."
- ☐ "Stop! Don't do that!"
- ☐ "No! Take your hand away from the stove. It's hot."
- ☐ "You can't do anything right!"
- ☐ "Why are you doing it that way?"
- ☐ "Okay, let's try to walk to mommy again."
- ☐ "Okay, let's walk to mommy again."
- ☐ "How can you be so stupid?"
- ☐ "Almost!"
- ☐ "Great, you did it!"
- ☐ "Just about!"
- ☐ "That was pretty close."
- ☐ "It can't be done that way."
- ☐ "You forgot something."
- ☐ "You didn't listen to me."
- ☐ "I meant like this."

Turn to page 18 in the HANDBOOK ➔

Chapter 1. GETTING STARTED
How Teachers Teach, continued

Today's date _____
Your child's
age today _____

You have been trying to teach your child to feed herself. She does fine when you put your hand over hers and help her feed herself, but you have tried for 2 weeks now to get her to hold the spoon herself. She won't do it, and you end up feeding her again. What's wrong?

- ☐ Child doesn't want to hold spoon
- ☐ Child cannot hold spoon without your help
- ☐ Child isn't ready to do it by herself
- ☐ You sometimes help her right away and sometimes you wait to help her until you get angry and close to tears

- ☐ Other: _____

_____

What can you do?

- ☐ Start by putting your hand on her wrist to help her, and then on her forearm
- ☐ Find out if she likes the feel of the spoon
- ☐ Put a foam haircurler on the spoon handle and see if she will hold the spoon then
- ☐ Nothing. She isn't ready to feed herself and you might as well give up now
- ☐ Find out if she holds other objects
- ☐ Find out if she brings anything to her mouth by herself

- ☐ Other: _____

_____

There is not one right answer to this question. You might try all of these at one time or another. Use your instincts about your child to help get over this hump, but don't make excuses for her. *Expect* that she can learn — and she most probably *will* learn.

You have now had a chance to think about what you want your child to learn. Use this space to write down today what you would like your child to learn during *the next six months.* Come back to this page from time to time, and see how your child is doing. You may find that your goals were way out of line — you may have chosen goals that *no* child could learn in six months. But at least you will start thinking in terms of goal, limits, and expectations — of where your child is today, and where she is going tomorrow.

Today's date: _____

Date 6 months from today: _____

My goals for _____
        (Child's name)

1. _____

_____

_____

2. _____

_____

_____

3. _____

_____

_____

4. _____

_____

_____

5. _____

_____

_____

6. _____

_____

_____

7. _____

_____

_____

8. _____

_____

_____

Turn to page 19 in the HANDBOOK ➡

Chapter 1. GETTING STARTED
Finding Help

The names and addresses of the three national organizations for parents of blind, visually impaired, and multiply handicapped children are listed again below. Use this chart to keep track of when you called or sent for information, and when you received it.

Organization	Date Contacted	How Contacted	Date of Response
American Council of the Blind—Parents c/o American Council of the Blind, Inc. 1211 Connecticut Avenue, N.W., Suite 506 Washington, D.C. 20036-2775 202-833-1251			
National Association for Parents of the Visually Impaired, Inc. P.O. Box 180806 Austin, Texas 78718 512-459-6651			
Parents of Blind Children Division National Federation of the Blind 1800 Johnson Street Baltimore, Maryland 21230 301-659-9314			

Turn to page 21 in the HANDBOOK

Chapter 1. GETTING STARTED
Community Resources

Today's date _____
Your child's
age today _____

Exploring your own community, make a list of possible services for your visually impaired or multiply handicapped child.

First, go to the yellow pages of your telephone book.

Look under "Schools."

Is your local school district listed? (If not, you may need to look in the white pages under the name of your hometown.)

Write the name and phone number here:

Name: _____

Address: _____

Phone: _____

Is there a separate number for "Special Education" or "Exceptional Students"?

If so, write that phone number here:

Special Education Phone: _____

Look through the rest of the schools listed. Are there any which say they accept handicapped children? If so, write them here:

Name: _____

Address: _____

Phone: _____

Name: _____

Address: _____

Phone: _____

Community Resources

Name: _____

Address: _____

Phone: _____

Name: _____

Address: _____

Phone: _____

Name: _____

Address: _____

Phone: _____

Name: _____

Address: _____

Phone: _____

Now, look under "Nursery Schools and Kindergartens."

Do any of those say they accept handicapped children?

If so, write them here:

Name: _____

Address: _____

Phone: _____

Name: _____

Address: _____

Phone: _____

Name: _____

Address: _____

Phone: _____

Name: _____

Address: _____

Phone: _____

Name: _____

Address: _____

Phone: _____

Name: _____

Address: _____

Phone: _____

Which is the closest nursery school to where you are living now?

Name: _____

Address _____

Phone: _____

Call this nursery school and ask:

What age children do you accept? _____

Have you ever had a handicapped child enrolled in the program?
☐ Yes
☐ No

Have you ever had a visually impaired child enrolled?
☐ Yes
☐ No

Look under "Social Service Organizations." Some organizations that might be helpful to you will have names like:

Association for Retarded Children
Association for the Education of Young Children
Association for the Visually Handicapped
Center for Family and Child Development
Center for Independent Living
Child Care Association
Child Guidance
Community Action Group
Day Care Council
Easter Seal Society
Family Day Service
Family Service
Industry for the Blind
The Lighthouse
National Foundation — March of Dimes
United Cerebral Palsy
United Way

If your child has a secondary handicap, you may find there is an organization just for that group of individuals:

Myasthenia Gravis Foundation, Inc.
Muscular Dystrophy Association, Inc.
Autism National Society

Community Resources

You may not have a use for these organizations now; then again, they may be able to give you some help. Use the next two pages to write down the names and addresses that you've found, so you can look them up again easily when needed.

Name: _____

Address:_____

Phone: _____

Name: _____

Address:_____

Phone: _____

Name: _____

Address:_____

Phone: _____

Name: _____

Address:_____

Phone: _____

Name: _____

Address:_____

Phone: _____

Name: _____

Address:_____

Phone: _____

Name: _____

Address: _____

Phone: _____

Name: _____

Address: _____

Phone: _____

Name: _____

Address: _____

Phone: _____

Name: _____

Address: _____

Phone: _____

Name: _____

Address: _____

Phone: _____

Name: _____

Address: _____

Phone: _____

Community Resources

Now try the white pages of your phone book. Some large city phone books have a set of blue pages in the back with government listings. If your book does, turn to those now.

If not, look up, first, the name of your town ("Clayton, Borough of" or "New Brunswick, City of") and then, the name of your county ("Fairfax, County of"). You can also look under your state ("Kansas, State of") and the "United States Government."

To find services that might be of help to you and your child, look at headings such as:

Board of Education
Children — Special Services
Day Care
Education
Handicapped
Mental Health Facilities
Social Security — Supplemental Security Income
Social Services
Superintendent of Schools
Welfare Board

Use this page and the next one to write down any numbers that you have found:

Name: _____

Address:_____

Phone: _____

Name: _____

Address:_____

Phone: _____

Name: _____

Address:_____

Phone: _____

Name: _____

Address:_____

Phone: _____

Name: _____

Address:_____

Phone: _____

Name: _____

Address: _____

Phone: _____

Name: _____

Address: _____

Phone: _____

Name: _____

Address: _____

Phone: _____

Name: _____

Address: _____

Phone: _____

Name: _____

Address: _____

Phone: _____

Name: _____

Address: _____

Phone: _____

Name: _____

Address: _____

Phone: _____

Name: _____

Address: _____

Phone: _____

Name: _____

Address: _____

Phone: _____

Turn to page 22 in the HANDBOOK ➤

Chapter 1. GETTING STARTED
Community Resources, continued

Today's date _____
Your child's
age today _____

Select an agency from the lists you have made on the previous pages. Call them and make arrangements to speak to them about your child. Use this page to keep a diary about your reactions to this process.

Name: _____

Address: _____

Phone: _____

Was the phone number correct?   ☐ Yes
                                 ☐ No

Were the people on the phone   ☐ Polite?
                               ☐ Rude?

Were they   ☐ Helpful?
            ☐ Not helpful?

Did you actually get through to anyone?   ☐ Yes
                                          ☐ No

Did the people you talked to give you their names, or did you have to ask what their names were?   ☐ They told me
                                                                                                   ☐ I had to ask

Were you put on hold?   ☐ Yes
                        ☐ No

Did they play music when you were on hold?   ☐ Yes
                                             ☐ No

Was anyone employed in the position you asked to speak to?   ☐ Yes
                                                             ☐ No

Did they switch you from person to person before you talked to someone who could answer your questions about services?   ☐ Yes
                                                                                                                        ☐ No

Did they offer help   ☐ Immediately?
                      ☐ At some future date?

Other comments about this telephone call: _____

_____

_____

_____

_____

_____

Turn to page 22 in the HANDBOOK

Chapter 1. GETTING STARTED
Preschool Programs

Today's date _____
Your child's
age today _____

To find out about your state's special education laws, write to:

(Name of your state) Department of Education
Consultant for the Visually Handicapped
Division for Exceptional Students
(State Capital), (State)

You want to ask:

1. At what age are public schools required to provide special
educational services for visually and multiply handicapped children?

_____
_____
_____

2. Are infant and preschool special educational services mandated
(required) or permissive (allowed)?

_____
_____
_____

3. What kinds of services are available for my child's age?

_____
_____
_____

4. How do I obtain services for my child?

_____
_____
_____

Also ask for any pamphlets or brochures on special education,
early childhood, and your legal rights.

Turn to page 23 in the HANDBOOK ➡

Chapter 1. GETTING STARTED
Preschool Programs, continued

Today's date _____
Your child's
age today _____

Contact the superintendent of your local school system. (Write the name, address, and phone number below.)

Name: _____

Address: _____

Phone: _____

Ask for the following information, and write the answers here:

1. What kinds of special eductional services are provided for handicapped infants and preschoolers?

_____

_____

_____

2. When can services be provided for *my* child?

_____

_____

_____

3. Whom should I contact to obtain these services?

_____

_____

_____

4. If the superintendent cannot provide services now, how does he or she plan to provide services later?

_____

_____

Turn to page 23 in the HANDBOOK

Chapter 1. GETTING STARTED
Finding Help

Today's date _____
Your child's
age today _____

**Organizations of Interest to Parents of Visually or
Multiply Handicapped Children**

There are a variety of agencies and organizations that provide information and assistance to you and your visually handicapped child on the national, state, and local level. For a comprehensive list of these agencies, ask your local librarian for a copy of the *Directory of Services for Blind and Visually Impaired Persons in the United States* (also available from the American Foundation for the Blind).

Organization	Date Contacted	How Contacted	Date of Response
Affiliated Leadership League of and for the Blind of America 1101 17th Street, N.W. Suite 803 Washington, D.C. 20036 202-833-0084	_____	_____	_____
Alexander Graham Bell Association for the Deaf 3417 Volta Place, N.W. Washington, D.C. 20007-2778 202-337-5220	_____	_____	_____
American Academy of Optometry 4330 East-West Highway Suite 1117 Bethesda, Maryland 20814 301-718-6500	_____	_____	_____
American Association of Ophthalmology 1101 Vermont Avenue, N.W. Suite 300 Washington, D.C. 20005 202-737-6652	_____	_____	_____
American Association on Mental Deficiency 5101 Wisconsin Avenue, N.W. Suite 405 Washington, D.C. 20016 202-686-5400	_____	_____	_____

Finding Help

Organization	Date Contacted	How Contacted	Date of Response
American Council of the Blind, Inc. 1155 15th Street, N.W. Suite 720 Washington, D.C. 20005 202-467-5081	_____	_____	_____
American Foundation for the Blind 15 West 16th Street New York, New York 10011 212-620-2000	_____	_____	_____
Regional Centers			
Eastern Regional Center (Connecticut, Delaware, District of Columbia, Maine, Maryland, Massachusetts, New Hampshire, New Jersey, New York, Pennsylvania, Rhode Island, Vermont, and Virginia) 1615 M Street, N.W. Suite 250 Washington, D.C. 20036 202-457-1487	_____	_____	_____
Midwest Regional Center (Illinois, Indiana, Iowa, Kentucky, Michigan, Minnesota, Missouri, Ohio, North Dakota, South Dakota, and Wisconsin) 20 North Wacker Drive Suite 1938 Chicago, Illinois 60606 312-269-0095	_____	_____	_____
Southeast Regional Center (Alabama, Florida, Georgia, Mississippi, North Carolina, Puerto Rico, South Carolina, Tennessee, Virgin Islands, and West Virginia) 100 Peachtree Street Suite 1016 Atlanta, Georgia 30303 404-525-2303	_____	_____	_____

Organization	Date Contacted	How Contacted	Date of Response
Southwest Regional Center (Arkansas, Colorado, Kansas, Louisiana, Montana, Nebraska, New Mexico, Oklahoma, Texas, and Wyoming) 260 Treadway Plaza Exchange Park Dallas, Texas 75235 214-352-7222	_____	_____	_____
Western Regional Center (Alaska, Arizona, California, Guam, Hawaii, Idaho, Nevada, Oregon, Utah, and Washington) 111 Pine Street Suite 725 San Francisco, California 94111 415-392-4845	_____	_____	_____
American Optometric Association 243 North Lindbergh Boulevard St. Louis, Missouri 63141 314-991-4100	_____	_____	_____
American Printing House for the Blind 1839 Frankfort Avenue Louisville, Kentucky 40206 502-895-2405	_____	_____	_____
American Speech-Language-Hearing Association 10801 Rockville Pike Rockville, Maryland 20852 301-897-5700	_____	_____	_____
Association for Education and Rehabilitation of the Blind and Visually Impaired 206 North Washington Stret Suite 320 Alexandria, Virginia 22314 703-548-1884	_____	_____	_____

Finding Help

Organization	Date Contacted	How Contacted	Date of Response
Association for Persons with Severe Handicaps 11201 Greenwood Avenue, North Seattle, Washington 98133 206-361-8870	_____	_____	_____
Association for Retarded Citizens 500 East Border Street Suite 300 Arlington, Texas 76010 817-261-6003	_____	_____	_____
Children's Defense Fund 122 C Street, N.W. Suite 400 Washington, D.C. 20001 202-628-8787	_____	_____	_____
Christian Education for the Blind, Inc. P.O. Box 6399 Fort Worth, Texas 76115 817-923-0603	_____	_____	_____
Christian Record Services 4444 South 52nd Street Lincoln, Nebraska 68506 402-488-0981	_____	_____	_____
Church of Jesus Christ of Latter-Day Saints Special Curriculum 50 East North Temple, 24th Floor Salt Lake City, Utah 84150 801-240-1000	_____	_____	_____
Council for Exceptional Children 1920 Association Drive Reston, Virginia 22091 703-620-3660 or 800-8456-CEC	_____	_____	_____

Organization	Date Contacted	How Contacted	Date of Response
Delta Gamma Foundation Executive Offices 3250 Riverside Drive Columbus, Ohio 43221 614-481-8169	_____	_____	_____
Epilepsy Foundation of America 4351 Garden City Drive Landover, Maryland 20785 301-459-3700	_____	_____	_____
Hadley School for the Blind 700 Elm Street Winnetka, Illinois 60093 312-446-8111 or 800-323-4238 (Reach Out and Teach for Parents)	_____	_____	_____
Howe Press Perkins School for the Blind 175 North Beacon Street Watertown, Massachusetts 02172 617-924-3434	_____	_____	_____
International Association of Lions Clubs 300 22nd Street Oak Brook, Illinois 60570 708-571-5466	_____	_____	_____
Jewish Braille Institute of America, Inc. 110 East 30th Street New York, New York 10016 212-889-2525	_____	_____	_____
Lutheran Braille Workers, Inc. 11735 Peach Tree Circle Yucaipa, California 92399 714-797-3093	_____	_____	_____

Finding Help

Organization	Date Contacted	How Contacted	Date of Response
March of Dimes Birth Defects Foundation 1275 Mamaroneck Avenue White Plains, New York 10602 914-428-7100	_____	_____	_____

National Accreditation Council for
  Agencies Serving the Blind and
  Visually Handicapped
232 Madison Avenue
Suite 907
New York, New York 10016
212-779-8080
	_____	_____	_____

National Association for Parents of the Visually Impaired 2180 Linway Drive Beloit, Wisconsin 53511-2720 608-362-4945 or 800-562-6265	_____	_____	_____
National Association for the Education of Young Children 1834 Connecticut Avenue, N.W. Washington, D.C. 20009 202-232-8777 or 800-424-2460	_____	_____	_____
National Association for Visually Handicapped 22 West 21st Street New York, New York 10010 212-889-3141	_____	_____	_____
National Braille Association 1290 University Avenue Rochester, New York 14607 716-473-0900	_____	_____	_____
National Children's Eye Care Foundation One Clinic Center, A3-108 9500 Euclid Avenue Cleveland, Ohio 44192 216-444-0488	_____	_____	_____

Organization	Date Contacted	How Contacted	Date of Response
National Easter Seal Society 2023 West Ogden Avenue Chicago, Illinois 60612 312-243-8400	_____	_____	_____
National Federation of the Blind 1800 Johnson Street Baltimore, Maryland 21230 301-659-9314	_____	_____	_____
National Information Center for Handicapped Children and Youth P.O. Box 1492 Washington, D.C. 20013 703-893-6061 or 800-999-5599	_____	_____	_____
National Newspatch Oregon School for the Blind 700 Church Street, S.E. Salem, Oregon 97301 503-378-3820	_____	_____	_____
National Society to Prevent Blindness 500 East Remington Road Schaumburg, Illinois 60173 312-843-2020	_____	_____	_____
Recording for the Blind, Inc. 20 Roszel Road Princeton, New Jersey 08540 609-452-0606	_____	_____	_____
RP Foundation Fighting Blindness (National Retinitis Pigmentosa Foundation) 1401 Mt. Royal Avenue Baltimore, Maryland 21217 301-225-9400	_____	_____	_____

Finding Help

Organization	Date Contacted	How Contacted	Date of Response
Sibling Information Network 991 Main Street Suite 3A East Hartford, CT 06108 203-282-7050	_____	_____	_____
United Cerebral Palsy Associations 1522 K Street, N.W. Suite 1112 Washington, D.C. 20005 202-371-0622	_____	_____	_____
Xavier Society for the Blind 154 East 23rd Street New York, New York 10010 212-473-7800	_____	_____	_____

UNITED STATES GOVERNMENT AGENCIES

| Consumer Product Safety Commission
Washington, D.C. 20207
301-504-0580 | _____ | _____ | _____ |

Organization	Date Contacted	How Contacted	Date of Response
National Institute on Disability and Rehabilitation Research 330 C Street, S.W. Washington, D.C. 20202 202-732-1134	_____	_____	_____
National Institutes of Health National Eye Institute 9000 Rockville Pike Building 31, Room 6A03 Bethesda, Maryland 20892 301-496-2234	_____	_____	_____
National Library Service for the Blind and Physically Handicapped The Library of Congress 1291 Taylor Street, N.W. Washington, D.C. 20542 202-707-5100 or 800-424-9100	_____	_____	_____
Office of Special Education Programs Early Childhood Education 400 Maryland Avenue, S.W. Switzer Building, Room 4617 Washington, D.C. 20202 202-732-1084	_____	_____	_____

Turn to page 27 in the HANDBOOK

TALKING IT OVER:

You, Your Family and the World

Today's date _____
Your child's
age today _____

Dealing with Your Child's Handicap

Many people have never had a friend or relative who is handicapped. How about you? Is your visually or multiply handicapped
child your first close contact with a handicapped person?

☐ Yes   ☐ No

If you answered "No," who is the handicapped person or persons
that you know — a friend or relative?

_____

_____

What is his or her handicapping condition?

_____

_____

Did it seem like a handicap to you, or was it something that really
didn't give your friend/relative much difficulty?

_____

_____

If your visually or multiply handicapped child is your first contact
with a handicapped person, how does that make you feel?
(Check all that apply.)

☐ Worried   ☐ Scared
☐ Curious   ☐ Confused
☐ Proud   ☐ Relieved that he is okay and not
☐ Concerned   unhealthy

☐ Other:_____

_____

_____

Dealing with Your Child's Handicap

Have you known anyone who was blind or visually handicapped?
If so, were they:

- ☐ Elderly
- ☐ Employed
- ☐ On welfare
- ☐ Well-dressed
- ☐ Frail
- ☐ Married
- ☐ Interesting
- ☐ Skittish
- ☐ Musical

- ☐ A child of school age
- ☐ Helpless
- ☐ Sloppy
- ☐ Handsome
- ☐ Independent
- ☐ Parents with children of their own
- ☐ Easy to talk to
- ☐ Self-confident
- ☐ Funny

If you have known blind or visually handicapped persons, what are
your general feelings about their abilities? Did anything about them
surprise you?

_____

_____

_____

_____

_____

◄ **Turn to page 34 in the HANDBOOK**

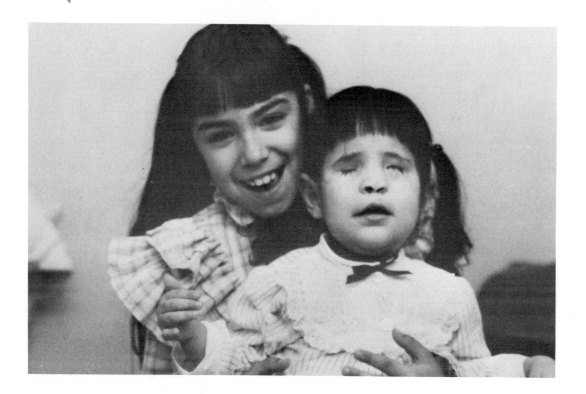

Chapter 2. TALKING IT OVER
Understanding Your Child's Vision

Today's date _____
Your child's
age today _____

Do you wear glasses?

☐ Yes   ☐ No

Why do you wear glasses? Describe your eye condition and what
your glasses do to help you see better:

_____

_____

_____

What is your visual acuity in:

Both eyes: _____

Right eye: _____   Left eye: _____

☐ Do not know

What is your child's eye condition?

_____

_____

Turn to page 36 in the HANDBOOK ➤

Chapter 2. TALKING IT OVER
Questions You Should Ask Your Eye Specialist

Today's date _____
Your child's
age today _____

Listed below are 15 questions that you will want to ask your eye specialist so that you can best understand your child's vision. If you already have the answers to these questions, please fill in the space underneath the questions with the answer as you understand it.

If you do not know some or all of the answers to these questions, take this REACHBOOK with you on your next visit to the eye specialist. You can write down the answers as you talk, or you can ask the eye specialist to answer the questions later in writing and then send them to you.

1. What caused my child's visual problem?

_____

_____

_____

2. Is this eye condition hereditary?

_____

_____

_____

3. Will my child's eye condition change?

_____

_____

_____

4. Where is the problem located?

_____

_____

_____

5. Do my child's pupils react to light?

_____

_____

_____

6. What is my child's tracking like?

_____

_____

_____

7. What is my child's central vision like?

_____

_____

_____

8. What is my child's field of vision like?

_____

_____

_____

9. What is my child's best viewing distance?

_____

_____

_____

10. How does this eye condition affect my child's mobility?

_____

_____

_____

11. Are my child's eyes sensitive to light?

_____

_____

_____

12. Does my child have light perception?

_____

_____

_____

13. Does my child have light projection?

_____

_____

_____

14. Will glasses or contact lenses help?

_____

_____

_____

Questions You Should Ask Your Eye Specialist

15. Will low vision aids help?

Turn to page 48 in the HANDBOOK

Chapter 2. TALKING IT OVER
Questions Your Eye Specialist Should Ask You

Today's date _____
Your child's
age today _____

Be prepared to answer these questions for your eye specialist:

1. Does your child hold his head in an unusual way? If so, describe it here:

_____

_____

_____

2. What does your child do when he first goes outside on a bright, sunny day? Does he do the same thing if he is in a room with a bright light? Describe your child's reactions below:

_____

_____

_____

3. Does your child reach?

☐ Yes   ☐ Not Yet

If "Yes," check each item below that describes her reaching behavior:

☐ Sees something across the room and moves toward it
☐ Always reaches for and gets what she wants
☐ Sometimes reaches too far, as though the object she is after is farther away than it really is
☐ Sometimes does not reach far enough, as though the object is closer than it really is
☐ Only reaches for things that are within 3 feet of her body
☐ Only reaches for objects located on her right side
☐ Only reaches for objects located on her left side
☐ Does not try to reach for moving objects
☐ Does try to reach for moving objects, but is unsuccessful
☐ Successfully reaches for moving objects
☐ Seems to prefer small objects
☐ Reaches more successfully to larger objects

4. What else have you noticed about your child's reaching behaviors?

_____

_____

_____

Questions Your Eye Specialist Should Ask You

5. Does your child hold objects close to his eyes or move up close to see things like the television?

☐ Usually   ☐ Sometimes   ☐ Never

If "Usually" or "Sometimes" does he do this with both eyes?

☐ Yes   ☐ No

or just with one eye?   ☐ Just the right eye
                         ☐ Just the left eye

What do you think this means?

_____

_____

_____

Did your eye specialist ask you any of these questions, or did you have to volunteer this information to him? Check the appropriate space below?

1. Does your child hold his head in an unusual way?

   ☐ Specialist asked
   ☐ You volunteered

2. What does your child do when she first goes outside on a bright sunny day?

   ☐ Specialist asked
   ☐ You volunteered

3. Does you child reach?

   ☐ Specialist asked
   ☐ You volunteered

4. Does your child hold objects close to her eyes or move up close to see things like the television?

   ☐ Specialist asked
   ☐ You volunteered

How do you rate the information given to you by your eye specialist?

☐ Excellent   ☐ Good   ☐ Fair   ☐ Poor

How do you rate what you have learned about your child's vision by observing him yourself?

☐ Excellent   ☐ Good   ☐ Fair   ☐ Poor

Turn to page 51 in the HANDBOOK

Today's date _____
Your child's
age today _____

Chapter 2. TALKING IT OVER
Your Child's Self-Concept

How would you describe *your* self-concept today?

☐ Pretty good   ☐ In bad shape
☐ Needs fixing   ☐ Terrific!

☐ Other: _____

_____

Check off any of the following words that describe how you see
yourself:

☐ Happy   ☐ Pleased
☐ Proud   ☐ Unsure
☐ Good-looking   ☐ Too fat
☐ Funny   ☐ Successful
☐ Friendly   ☐ Well-dressed
☐ Tired   ☐ Anxious
☐ Lazy   ☐ Good parent

☐ Other: _____

_____

_____

What kind of a day has it been for *your child*?

☐ Frustrating   ☐ Successful
☐ Learned something new   ☐ Cried a lot
☐ Ate lunch himself   ☐ Forgot his name
☐ Had a toileting accident ☐ Played with friends
☐ Helped you around the house ☐ Dressed himself
☐ Full of punishment   ☐ Visited the doctor
☐ Annoying   ☐ Full of laughter

☐ Other: _____

_____

_____

Turn to page 53 in the HANDBOOK ➜

Chapter 2. TALKING IT OVER
Shaping Your Child's Personality

Today's date _____
Your child's
age today _____

Did your mother or father have a favorite saying that you remember hearing from the time you were a child?

☐ Yes   ☐ No   ☐ Do not remember

If "Yes," what was it?

_____

Many adults promise themselves that they will "do things differently" when they are parents. How about you? Did you want to be different from, or just like your parents?

☐ Different from my parents
☐ Just like my parents

Is there something your parents did for you as a child that you thought was so great that you want to do it for your children, too? If so, what was it?

_____

_____

_____

Is there something your parents did that you promised yourself you would *never* do? If so, what was it?

_____

_____

_____

When you were a child was there an adult in your life whom you especially admired?

☐ Yes   ☐ No

Who was it? _____

Why did you admire him or her? _____

_____

_____

Turn to page 54 in the HANDBOOK ➡

Chapter 2. TALKING IT OVER
Shaping Your Child's Personality, continued

Today's date _____
Your child's
age today _____

Children can take an active part in life, regardless of how visually
or multiply handicapped they are. One of the ways you can help
your child do this is by giving him choices. Check off the choices
your child has been allowed to make—or participate in—today:

☐ What clothes to wear
☐ What time to get up out of bed
☐ What time to take a nap
☐ Which books to look at
☐ What to eat for breakfast or lunch
☐ What to eat for a snack
☐ What to drink when he is thirsty
☐ Going outside
☐ Going to school
☐ Riding in the car

☐ Other choices: _____

_____

_____

Do you think your child is too young to make any of the choices
listed above?

☐ Yes
☐ No
☐ Not sure

Do you think your child is too handicapped to make any of the
choices listed above?

☐ Yes
☐ No
☐ Not sure

Why do you think so? Is it because your child is so handicapped
that he has no way of telling you what his choice is?

_____

_____

_____

Shaping Your Child's Personality

Remember that your handicapped child may take longer to respond if you ask a question or try to involve him in making choices. He also might give you only a slight indication of what his choice is — a movement of his foot, perhaps, or a blink of the eyes. Observe your child carefully. He may be giving you signals even though he has no way of telling you.

And give him the benefit of the doubt—always give him the choice even if he does not seem to respond. Some day he might.

Turn to page 57 in the HANDBOOK

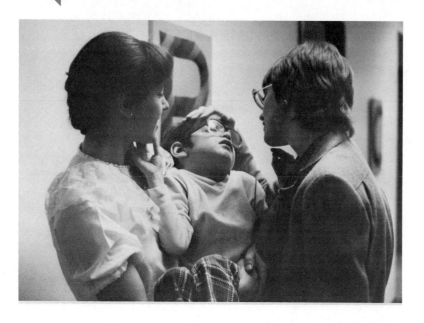

Chapter 2. TALKING IT OVER
Dealing with Your Child's Behavior

Today's date _____
Your child's
age today _____

Take 5 minutes out of your busy schedule, sit down, and observe your child. Take notes on what he is doing — whether he is playing with toys, friends, or another adult. Try to divide the things that happen into *cause, action,* and *consequence.* As you observe, write your notes below:

CAUSE (What made something happen)

_____

_____

ACTION (What actually happened)

_____

_____

CONSEQUENCE (What resulted, or what the action led to)

_____

_____

Looking back at your notes are you able to find any patterns either in what *causes* your child to do something, or what happens *after* she does it? If so, what patterns did you see:

_____

_____

_____

_____

The causes-action-consequence model can be used to teach as well as to change behavior. For example, suppose you want to teach your child to put away her toys. "Putting away toys" is the *action*; you can decide what the *cause* and *consequence* will be. The *cause* might be a simple verbal reminder—"Lauren, put your toys away." Or, because of your child's needs, *cause* might be a combinantion of a verbal reminder with a hand-over-hand procedure to help her put them away. As a *consequence*, you might choose to praise her ("Good work, Lauren — you put all your toys away!"), give her a hug, or read her a story. If you do this once each day, and consistently use the same *causes* and *consequences*, your child's chance of learning to put away her toys herself are very good.

Now, identify a skill that you would like your child to learn. This is the *action* that you want your child to do. Write it here:

_____

_____

_____

Dealing with Your Child's Behavior

Now, what can *you* do to *cause* that action to happen?

_____

_____

_____

And what will *you* do for your child as a *consequence* or reward for trying (and eventually succeeding)?

_____

_____

_____

_____

_____

Changing Behavior

If you want to *change* your child's behavior — either because it is unattractive, rude, annoying, or whatever — you use the same *cause-action-consequence* model, but you look at it a little differently.

1. Decide what it is you want to change. For example, your multiply handicapped 4-year-old crawls over to the refrigerator and cries when she is thirsty, and you would like her to stop crying and use some other way of asking you for a drink.

2. Then, keep a diary of what happens immediately before and immediately after she crawls over to the refrigerator and cries. It might look something like this:

CAUSE (What made it happen)

SISTER HITS LAUREN

_____

ACTION (What actually happened)

LAUREN CRAWLS OVER TO REFRIGERATOR AND CRIES

CONSEQUENCE (What resulted, or what the action led to)

DAD GIVES LAUREN A DRINK

_____

CAUSE (What made it happen)

DAD LEAVES ROOM

_____

ACTION (What actually happened)

LAUREN CRAWLS OVER TO REFRIGERATOR
AND CRIES

CONSEQUENCE (What resulted, or what the action led to)

MOM GIVES LAUREN A DRINK

CAUSE (What made it happen)

DAD TALKING ON TELEPHONE

ACTION (What actually happened)

SAME ACTION AS ABOVE

CONSEQUENCE (What resulted, or what the action led to)

MOM GIVES DRINK

CAUSE (What made it happen)

SISTER IS WRESTLING WITH MOM ON
THE FLOOR

ACTION (What actually happened)

SAME

CONSEQUENCE (What resulted, or what the action led to)

MOM GIVES DRINK

If you examine the diary, two things stand out: (1) Lauren always gets a drink when she cries; and (2) it looks like what Lauren really wants is someone to pay attention to her. Right before she crawls over to the refrigerator, the people around her become busy with something or someone *other than* Lauren.

Now that you have analyzed the situation, you can either (1) change the consequence — Lauren's crying is too successful right now, and she should *not* be given a drink when she crawls over to the refrigerator and cries; or (2) change the cause — by stopping her before she gets to the refrigerator and showing her how to do something else. Or you could teach her the sign for "drink," or teach her how

Dealing with Your Child's Behavior

to get a drink for herself. But remember — your notetaking has told you that getting a drink is not really Lauren's purpose.

The next few pages have been placed in your REACHBOOK for those times when you need to look more closely at your child's behavior. Use them as you need to, and make your own if you run out of these.

CAUSE (What made it happen)

_____

_____

ACTION (What actually happened)

_____

_____

CONSEQUENCE (What resulted, or what the action led to)

_____

_____

CAUSE (What made it happen)

_____

_____

ACTION (What actually happened)

_____

_____

CONSEQUENCE (What resulted, or what the action led to)

_____

_____

CAUSE (What made it happen)

_____

_____

ACTION (What actually happened)

_____

_____

CONSEQUENCE (What resulted, or what the action led to)

_____

_____

CAUSE (What made it happen)

_____

_____

ACTION (What actually happened)

_____

_____

CONSEQUENCE (What resulted, or what the action led to)

_____

_____

CAUSE (What made it happen)

_____

_____

ACTION (What actually happened)

_____

_____

CONSEQUENCE (What resulted, or what the action led to)

_____

_____

CAUSE (What made it happen)

_____

_____

ACTION (What actually happened)

_____

_____

CONSEQUENCE (What resulted, or what the action led to)

_____

_____

Dealing with Your Child's Behavior

CAUSE (What made it happen)

_____

_____

ACTION (What actually happened)

_____

_____

CONSEQUENCE (What resulted, or what the action led to)

_____

_____

CAUSE (What made it happen)

_____

_____

ACTION (What actually happened)

_____

_____

CONSEQUENCE (What resulted, or what the action led to)

_____

_____

CAUSE (What made it happen)

_____

_____

ACTION (What actually happened)

_____

_____

CONSEQUENCE (What resulted, or what the action led to)

_____

_____

CAUSE (What made it happen)

_____

_____

ACTION (What actually happened)

_____

_____

CONSEQUENCE (What resulted, or what the action led to)

_____

_____

CAUSE (What made it happen)

_____

_____

ACTION (What actually happened)

_____

_____

CONSEQUENCE (What resulted, or what the action led to)

_____

_____

Turn to page 60 in the HANDBOOK ➤

Chapter 2. TALKING IT OVER
Why it Seems Harder When Your Child is Handicapped

Today's date _____
Your child's
age today _____

Grandparents are not the only ones who have reactions to your family now that a visually or multiply handicapped child is part of it. Close friends and neighbors may have similar feelings.

For each typical reaction listed below, place a check mark in the column headed "Grandparents" if either your parents or your in-laws have done it; place a check mark in the column headed "Friends" if your friends have done it; and place a check mark in the column headed "Neighbors" if you think one or more of your neighbors have done it.

	Grandparents	Friends	Neighbors
Avoid visiting	☐	☐	☐
Avoid asking about your handicapped child	☐	☐	☐
Tell you that you expect too much from your child	☐	☐	☐
Tell you that you are mean to your child	☐	☐	☐
Offer to take your child overnight or for a weekend	☐	☐	☐
Seem depressed when around your child	☐	☐	☐
Seem to pity your child	☐	☐	☐
Drive you and your child to therapy or infant class	☐	☐	☐
Buy baby toys as gifts long after your child is a baby	☐	☐	☐
Think that your child is not doing as much as he should be doing at his age	☐	☐	☐

One of your friends who comes over to visit a lot always looks so sad when talking about your child and says things like:

"It must be so hard for you!"
"Poor child!"
"If only she could see!"

Your child is usually in the same room during these visits. What do you say to this person?

_____

_____

_____

_____

A stranger comes up to you in the store, starts talking baby talk to your 3-year-old, and says, "Oh, she's dreaming. Isn't that sweet?" when your child is really laughing and smiling back at her — but with her eyelids closed.

Do you tell this stranger that your child is visually impaired, or do you let it go? Why or why not?

Turn to page 64 in the HANDBOOK

Chapter 2. TALKING IT OVER
Family Interactions

Today's date _____
Your child's
age today _____

Describe a typical day in your life. The questions below will help
you:

What time did you get up? _____

What time did your child or children wake up? _____

Did you make breakfast, or did someone make it for you?

☐ I made it
☐ Someone else made it

Did you make breakfast just for yourself, or for your entire family?

☐ For myself
☐ For the entire family

How many times did you leave the house? _____

How many errands did you run, and where did you go? List each
one separately:

_____

_____

_____

_____

_____

_____

_____

_____

_____

_____

Have you had a chance to relax or take a nap today?

☐ Yes   ☐ No

Did you go to your child's school or infant program?

☐ Yes   ☐ No

And what happened while you were there?

_____

_____

_____

_____

_____

What did you do for lunch?

_____

_____

What did you do for dinner?

_____

_____

What television programs have you watched today?

_____

_____

_____

_____

_____

What time did your child or children go to bed? _____

Did you help them get ready for bed?

☐ Yes   ☐ No

How did you help them?

_____

_____

_____

Did you have any time alone with your spouse or partner?

☐ Yes
☐ No

Did you talk to anyone on the telephone?

☐ Yes
☐ No

How many telephone calls did you make? _____

Were they personal, household-connected, or child-connected?
How many of each:

☐ Personal _____
☐ Household-connected _____
☐ Child-connected _____

What time will you go to bed? _____

Family Interactions

Use this space to write anything else that you typically do every day:

_____

_____

_____

_____

_____

_____

_____

_____

_____

◄ **Turn to page 66 in the HANDBOOK**

Chapter 2. TALKING IT OVER
Family Interactions, continued

Today's date _____
Your child's
age today _____

What counseling services are available in your community?

_____

_____

_____

If you have not yet completed REACHBOOK pages 34–42, do them now. This should help you find some counseling services.

Select one of the agencies you found, call them, and ask if they provide respite care for families of handicapped children, or if they can refer you to an agency that does.

Any luck?   ☐ Yes
            ☐ No
            ☐ Maybe

Referred to: _____

Telephone: _____

Write the names and telephone numbers of your regular child-sitters here, where you can easily find them. If you do not have a regular sitter, or are having trouble finding someone to stay with your child, try asking a nurses' association, another parent in your preschool group, or call a nearby college or university.

Name   **Telephone Number**

_____   _____

_____   _____

_____   _____

Turn to page 68 in the HANDBOOK

Chapter 2. TALKING IT OVER
Your Rights as Parents

The right to feel angry

The right to seek another opinion

The right to privacy

The right to keep trying

The right to stop trying

The right to set limits

The right to be a parent

The right to be unenthusiastic

The right to be annoyed with your child

The right to time off

The right to be the expert-in-charge

The right to dignity

TAKING OFF:

Motor Development

Today's date _____
Your child's
age today _____

Guidelines for Teaching Your Child

List some of the activities you do to help take your mind off your
feelings of frustration:

_____

_____

_____

_____

_____

_____

_____

_____

_____

_____

What makes you frustrated? (Check all that apply.)

☐ Trying to teach my child to crawl
☐ Trying to teach my child to walk
☐ Feeding my child
☐ Toilet-training my child
☐ Not being able to go back to work
☐ Having to go back to work

☐ Other: _____

_____

Turn to page 81 in the HANDBOOK →

Chapter 3. TAKING OFF
Guidelines for Teaching Your Child, continued

Today's date _____
Your child's
age today _____

What are some of the things you do for your child now that your child may be able to do for herself?

_____

_____

_____

_____

_____

_____

_____

_____

_____

Why are you doing these things?

☐ Takes too much time   ☐ Like to do it
☐ Child cannot do it independently ☐ Want child to look perfect
☐ Child has tantrums if I don't

☐ Other: _____

_____

Turn to page 82 in the HANDBOOK ➡

Chapter 3. TAKING OFF
Learning to Move

Today's date _____
Your child's
age today _____

Here are two motor skills, one that uses large muscles, and one that uses small muscles. Which one do children normally learn first?

☐ Writing
☐ Rolling over

Here are another two motor skills. Which one do children learn first?

☐ Turning head
☐ Walking

In the following sets of two skills, mark the skill that children usually learn first:

☐ Putting arms over head to play "So big!"
☐ Stacking blocks

☐ Playing patty-cake
☐ Kicking a ball

☐ Banging a toy
☐ Picking up a raisin

Now try doing six skills at once. Number the following motor skills in the order in which children are usually able to do them:*

☐ Rolling over
☐ Turning head
☐ Walking
☐ Writing
☐ Stacking blocks
☐ Putting arms over head to play "So big!"

Turn to page 85 in the HANDBOOK

Chapter 3. TAKING OFF
Learning Stages

Today's date _____
Your child's
age today _____

Listed below are groups of three motor skills. In each box, mark which skill is first *learned* or *gained*; which has been *maintained*; and which shows the child has *applied* the skill. Use these letters:

G = Gained
M = Maintained
A = Applied

The first one has been done for you. Children first learn to grasp a rattle; they *maintain* their grasping skills in order to hold onto a crayon; and they *apply* that skill when learning to write.

_M_ Holding crayon
_A_ Writing alphabet
_G_ Grasping rattle

___ Standing
___ Skipping
___ Running

___ Sitting
___ Crawling
___ Rolling over

___ Putting on socks
___ Tying bow
___ Putting on shoes

___ Turning wrist
___ Drinking with cup
___ Opening jar

___ Walking
___ Running
___ Standing

___ Pulling to stand
___ Cruising (walking while holding onto furniture)
___ Crawling

___ Recognizing mommy's voice
___ Says "mama car"
___ Says "mama"

Turn to page 86 in the HANDBOOK

Chapter 3. TAKING OFF
Assessment of Reflexes

Today's date _____
Your child's
age today _____

Check your child for an asymmetrical tonic neck reflex (ATNR):

Place child on back.
Turn child's head to one side.
What happens? (Check all that apply.)

☐ Arm straightens on side toward which head was turned
☐ Arm opposite from head turn bends
☐ Leg on same side as head turn straightens
☐ Leg opposite from head turn bends
☐ Child cries

Have you seen your child in an ATNR position before, when you
haven't tried turning the head?
☐ Yes
☐ No

Assessment of Reflexes

Check your child for a symmetrical tonic neck reflex (STNR), and a Landau or extension reflex at the same time:

Place child tummy-down on your knee, or support child in air so that arms and legs are free. Make sure your child is balanced and will not fall out of your grasp.

What happens?
☐ Head comes up
☐ Legs straighten ⎤———————— This is the Landau

Push child's head down gently.

What happens?
☐ Legs bend at knees ⎤———————— This is the Landau
☐ Arms bend at elbows ⎦
☐ Legs straighten out ———————— This is an STNR

If head did not come up, lift child's head yourself.

What happens?
☐ Arms straighten ⎤
☐ Legs bend at knees ⎦———————— This is an STNR

**Landau reflex:
Head up, both arms
and legs straight.**

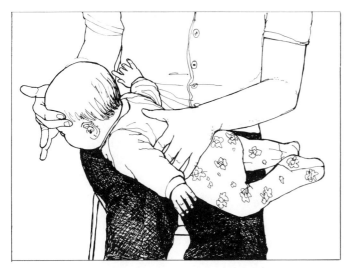

Symmetrical tonic rack relex (STNR): Head up, arms straight, legs bent.

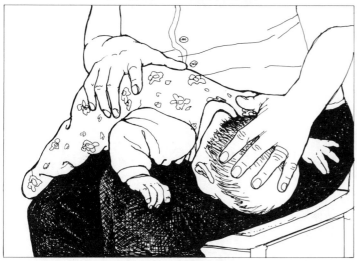

Symmetrical tonic neck reflex: Head down, arms bent, leg straight.

Maybe your child is already too old for these reflexes, and they have already disappeared. What do you think?

☐ Yes, too old
☐ No
☐ Not sure

What reflexes did you find that your child had?

☐ ATNR
☐ STNR
☐ Landau
☐ None

Mark the results of your reflex assessment on the Motor Progress Chart on page 95 of this REACHBOOK.

If your child is older than 9 to 12 months old and still shows these reflexes, be sure to ask your doctor about it.

Turn to page 92 in the HANDBOOK

Chapter 3. TAKING OFF
Muscle Tone Assessment

Today's date _____
Your child's
age today _____

Does your child's body feel like yours?
- ☐ Yes
- ☐ No
- ☐ Not sure

Does your child's body feel like a rag doll?
- ☐ Yes
- ☐ No
- ☐ Not sure

Does your child's body feel like a Barbie doll (stiff, moving only
at elbows and legs, if at all)?
- ☐ Yes
- ☐ No
- ☐ Not sure

How is your child's muscle tone?
- ☐ Good, feels just right
- ☐ Too loose — hypotonic
- ☐ Too tight — hypertonic

Turn to page 93 in the HANDBOOK

Chapter 3. TAKING OFF
Assessment of Balance

Today's date _____
Your child's
age today _____

Lay your child on his tummy.

What happens?   **Type of Balance**
☐ Lifts head; hands do not touch floor
☐ Lifts head; hands on floor; arms bent   HEAD
☐ Lifts head; hands on floor; arms straight
☐ Lifts head and shoulders; hands on floor; arms   SHOULDER
   straight
☐ Lifts head, shoulders, and trunk; hands on floor; TRUNK
   arms straight

Place your child in a sitting position without back support.

What happens?
☐ Falls forward
☐ Falls forward, but catches self with hands
☐ Sits with back straight; arms held up and bent
   at elbow
☐ Sits with back straight; uses hands to play with toys TRUNK
☐ Moves from sitting to crawling position

Place your child upright on his feet.

What happens?
☐ Legs bend; you must hold him up
☐ Takes some weight on feet
☐ Takes most weight on feet, but holds onto your
   hands
☐ Takes weight on feet; holds on with only one hand
☐ Stands alone, does not hold onto furniture or   STANDING
   your hands
☐ Walks, holds on with two hands
☐ Walks, holds on with one hand
☐ Walks alone, arms held at shoulder level, feet   WALKING
   wide apart
☐ Walks alone, arms lowered, feet close together

Does your child do any of these?
☐ Stands on one foot
☐ Runs
☐ Skips
☐ Jumps   MOVING
☐ Stoops to pick something up from floor, then
   stands up again
☐ Pulls or pushes toys while walking

Assessment of Balance

What kind of balance did you find that your child had?
- ☐ Head
- ☐ Shoulders
- ☐ Trunk
- ☐ Standing
- ☐ Walking
- ☐ Moving

Mark the results of your balance assessment on the Motor Progress Chart on page 95 of this REACHBOOK.

Turn to page 95 in the HANDBOOK

Chapter 3. TAKING OFF
Assessment of Rotation

Today's date _____
Your child's
age today _____

Have you seen your child:
☐ Turn her head when lying on her back?
☐ Turn her head when lying on her tummy?
☐ Hold her head off the floor and turn it when lying on her tummy?

Place your child on her side on the floor on a blanket. Make sure her arm is free.

What happens?
☐ Nothing
☐ Child rolls to back
☐ Child rolls to tummy

When your child is lying on her back, can you get her to roll to her side by talking to her or using a toy?
☐ Usually
☐ Sometimes
☐ Not yet

Does she roll all the way over to her tummy?
☐ Usually
☐ Sometimes
☐ Not yet

Place your child on her tummy and try to get her to roll all the way over onto her back.

Can she do it?
☐ Usually
☐ Sometimes
☐ Not yet

Place your child on the floor, if she can sit alone without help. Observe her for a few minutes.

What happens?
☐ Sits; spends most of time trying to keep her balance
☐ Sits; plays with toys in front of her
☐ Sits; reaches around for toys on sides and in back of her
☐ Moves out of sitting position and lies on tummy
☐ Moves out of sitting and starts to crawl on all fours (hands and knees)
☐ Moves out of sitting and starts to crawl on hands, knees, and forehead
☐ Sits; leans forward; sits up again

Assessment of Rotation

Now, place your child in a sitting position, but close to something she can use to pull herself up (like the playpen or the couch).

What happens?
☐ Moves out of sitting and pulls self to kneeling
☐ Moves out of sitting and pulls self to standing
☐ Nothing yet

If your child is standing, does she do any of the following?
☐ Cruises (walks holding onto furniture)
☐ Stands; holds on with one hand; reaches with other hand
☐ Stands; holds on with one hand, bends and picks something up off floor with other hand
☐ Stands; moves into sitting position while holding on
☐ Stands and *falls* down to sitting position
☐ Stands; moves into sitting without holding on
☐ Stands; turns around to face you when you call her; holds on with one hand

Does your child crawl?
☐ Yes
☐ Not yet

Does your child crawl like this?

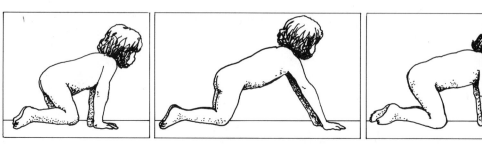

Or like this?

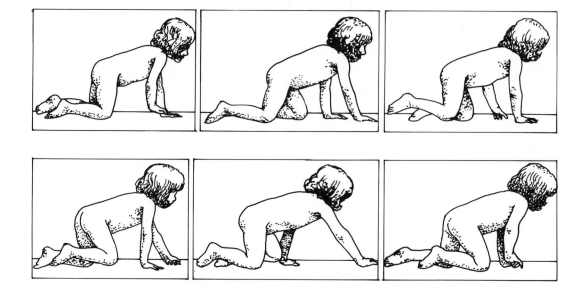

Assessment of Rotation

Which statement best describes how your child crawls?
☐ Pulls self forward with arms; tummy touches floor
☐ Uses hands and knees
☐ Arms move forward together, then brings both knees
  forward together
☐ Opposite arms and legs move forward at the same time
☐ Uses hands, knees, and forehead
☐ Goes backward
☐ Crawls; uses one hand to reach for toy
☐ Crawls; stops when you call her; moves arm toward back
  and turns to face you
☐ Sits; uses feet to pull self forward

Have you seen your child climb into an adult-size chair by herself,
turn around, and sit?
  ☐ Yes
  ☐ Not yet

What kind of rotation did you find that your child had?
☐ Head
☐ Shoulders
☐ Trunk
☐ Hip

Mark the results of your rotation assessment on the
Motor Progress Chart on page 96 of this REACHBOOK.

Turn to page 106 in the HANDBOOK ➜

Chapter 3. TAKING OFF
Assessment of Protective Reactions

Today's date _____
Your child's
age today _____

Does your child startle?
☐ Yes, easily
☐ Yes, but only to loud noises
☐ Not much
☐ Not at all

Place your child in a sitting position on the floor. Gently push him forward, just enough to lose his balance.

Does he stick out his hands and arms to catch himself?
☐ Yes
☐ Tries to
☐ Not yet

Sit behind your child, keeping him in a sitting position, and gently push him to the right.

Does he stick out his right arm and catch himself with his right hand?
☐ Yes
☐ Starts to, but does not quite do it
☐ Not yet

Now gently push him to the left.

Does he stick out his left arm and catch himself with his left hand?
☐ Yes
☐ Starts to, but does not quite do it
☐ Not yet

Now gently pull his shoulders toward you, again just enough to throw him off balance.

Does he:
☐ Stick one arm out and catch himelf?
☐ Stick two arms out and catch himself?
☐ Start to catch himself, but not quite make it?
☐ Not even try to catch himself, and you have to catch him
   to keep him from hurting himself?

What kind of protection reactions did you find that your child had?
☐ None yet
☐ Front protection
☐ Right side protection
☐ Left side protection
☐ Back protection

Mark the results of your assessment of protective reactions on the
Motor Progress Chart on page 96 of this REACHBOOK.

Turn to page 109 in the HANDBOOK

Chapter 3. TAKING OFF
Motor Progress Chart

Listed in the left column are all the movements discussed so far.
Use this chart to keep track of:

1. When you first looked to see if your child could do the skill ("Date Assessed")

2. Whether or not your child could do the skill on that date ("Yes, Child Does" or "Child Does Not Do Yet")

3. When you started to work with your child on the skill ("Date Began To Work On")

4. When your child begins to *gain* the skill ("Date Child Does With Help"), and

5. When your child really showed *maintenance* of the skill ("Date Child Does alone")

Movements	Date Assessed	Yes Child Does	Child Does Not Do Yet	Date Began To Work On	Date Child Does With Help	Date Child Does Alone
REFLEXES: ANTR						
STNR						
Landau						
BALANCE: Lies on tummy, lifts head						
Lies on tummy, pushes on hands, lifts head and shoulders						
Lies on tummy, pushes on hands, lifts head, shoulders, and chest						
Sits, leans forward on hands						
Sits up, without support						
Sits alone, plays with toys						
Takes weight on feet when placed in standing position						
Stands, holds on with two hands						
Stands, holds on with one hand						
Stands, without holding on						
Walks, holds on with two hands						
Walks, holds on with one hand						

Motor Progress Chart

Movements	Date Assessed	Yes Child Does	Child Does Not Do Yet	Date Began To Work On	Date Child Does With Help	Date Child Does Alone
Walks, without holding on						
Stoops to pick up from floor, returns to standing						
Pulls, pushes toys while walking						
Runs						
Stands on one foot						
Jumps						
ROTATION: Turns head						
Rolls side to back						
Rolls back to side						
Rolls back to tummy						
Rolls tummy to back						
Sits, reaches for toys behind						
Moves from sitting to tummy						
Moves from sitting to crawling						
Sits, leans forward, sits up again						
Moves from sitting to kneeling						
Moves from kneeling to standing						
Cruises holding onto furniture						
Moves from standing to sitting						
Crawls						
Climbs into adult chair, turns and sits						
PROTECTIVE REACTIONS: Catches self when falling forward						
Catches self when falling left						
Catches self when falling right						
Catches self when falling back						

Turn to page 113 in the HANDBOOK

PICKING UP:

Using One's Hands to Learn About the World

Today's date _____
Your child's
age today _____

The Motor Development Process

In this chapter you will be reading about fine motor development.
The basic process of motor development, whether it involves the
whole body or parts of the body, is always the same.

Draw an arrow between the word in column A and the word in
column B to best describe how this process works. Make sure your
arrow points in the right direction: **what comes first to what comes
last.**

Column A	Column B
Large	Small
Toe	Head
Arms & legs	Trunk
Simple	Complex

That was probably easy. Now, in the following pairs of skills,
decide which one is learned by children *first*, and which one is
learned *later*. For each pair, number the skill learned first as #1, and
the skill that is learned later as #2.

____ Claps hands together.
____ Writes name

____ Holds 2 cubes (one in each
hand) and bangs them together.
____ Builds a tower of cubes

____ Pulls string on toys
____ Pushes up on hands
while lying on tummy.

____ Throws ball.
____ Pushes keys down on braille
writer

____ Strings beads
____ Points with index finger.

____ "Chops" with scissors.
____ Cuts out square with scissors,
more or less cutting along line

____ Turns pages of book, one
page at a time
____ Turns several pages of book at
a time.

____ Prints letters
____ Scribbles.

The Motor Development Process

____ Turns doorknob

____ Holds, drinks from, and
returns cup to table.

How did you do? Check your work: **The skills that are followed by a period are the ones that are learned *first* in each pair.** If you disagree with any of these, try acting them out yourself. Sometimes it's easier to understand when you go through the movements yourself. If you still have a question, write it here:

_____

_____

_____

_____

Turn to page 118 in the HANDBOOK

Chapter 4. PICKING UP
The Importance of Weight-Bearing

Today's date _____
Your child's
age today _____

Even though you may already have tried this as part of the balance assessment in the "Taking Off" chapter of your REACHBOOK, please try this again: **Place your child on his tummy. What happens?**

Lifts:
- [ ] No body parts
- [ ] Head
- [ ] Shoulders
- [ ] Upper chest
- [ ] Trunk (shoulders to waist)

Hands are:
- [ ] Fisted
- [ ] Partially open
- [ ] Completely open
- [ ] Fingers spread
- [ ] Thumb tucked under
- [ ] Thumb spread out
- [ ] Placed directly below shoulders
- [ ] Placed slightly in front of shoulders

Arms are:
- [ ] Bent tightly at elbows
- [ ] Close to sides of body
- [ ] Bent slightly
- [ ] Straightened out
- [ ] Fully extended

Based on what you saw your baby do and the answers you checked above, does your child **bear weight** on her hands yet?

- [ ] Yes
- [ ] No, not yet

Does you child **shift** weight — that is, bear weight on one side and hand while doing something with the other hand?

- [ ] Yes
- [ ] No, not yet

Now look at what your child is doing with his hands. Check *all* the things you have seen your child do today.

- [ ] Hold one object in each hand
- [ ] Bang two objects together
- [ ] Pat toys, people, books, or table top
- [ ] Take an object in one hand and move it into the other
- [ ] Stack blocks or cookies
- [ ] Put things in containers and dump them out
- [ ] Zip and unzip zippers
- [ ] Button and unbutton
- [ ] Hands are slightly open
- [ ] Hands are fisted
- [ ] Poke holes with the index finger
- [ ] Scribble with crayon or pencil
- [ ] Put large-piece puzzles together
- [ ] Turn pages of books, several pages at a time
- [ ] Turn individual pages of books one at time
- [ ] Eat with fingers
- [ ] Eat with spoon or fork
- [ ] Tie shoes
- [ ] Grasp objects reflexively (hand closes tightly as soon as something touches palm of hand)

The Importance of Weight-Bearing

Okay, now you know something about how your child is using his hands. Now look more closely at his hand as he holds a small toy (a block or ring, or rattle). Look at the palm, fingers, and thumb separately and check all that apply.

Palm:

☐ Not used

☐ Palm squeezes against fingers

☐ Entire palm used

Fingers:

☐ Object held by fingers

☐ Fingers squeeze against palm

☐ Fingers closest to thumb do most of holding

☐ Index finger sticks out

☐ Index finger directly opposed to thumb tip

Thumb:

☐ Not used yet

☐ Moves sideways toward fingers

☐ Moves toward middle of index finger

☐ Moves toward tip of index finger

☐ Thumb directly opposed to index finger

Turn to page 120 in the HANDBOOK

Chapter 4. PICKING UP
Assessment of Grasp

Today's date _____
Your child's
age today _____

Based on what you have read about grasp, what type of grasp do
you think your child uses most of the time?

☐ Reflexive grasp
☐ Raking grasp
☐ Palmar, or squeeze grasp
☐ Whole-hand grasp
☐ Scissors grasp
☐ Forefinger grasp
☐ Pincer grasp (with wrist supported on table)
☐ Pincer grasp (without wrist support)

Give your child a wooden block. What happens? Check *all* that apply:

☐ Does not hold block   ☐ Thumb is not used

☐ Pressure is in finger   ☐ Palm is used

☐ Thumb is used   ☐ Palm is not used

Now give your child some pieces of dry cereal. What happens?
Check *all* that apply:

☐ "Rakes" up pieces, using fingers   ☐ Uses thumb and index fingers
   against fingers

☐ Holds piece against side of index   ☐ Holds piece at tip of index fingers
   fingers

☐ Holds piece against side of thumb   ☐ Holds piece at tip of thumb or
                                              on thumb pad

☐ Holds piece against underside (or
   palm side) of index finger

Now, give your child a crayon and piece of paper. How does your
child hold the crayon?

_____

_____

_____

Does your child do anything with the crayon? What?

_____

_____

_____

Assessment of Grasp

The chart on the next page summarizes the different types of grasps that children use. As you look at each column, decide which block best describes your child. Look at the "strength" column first, then color in the block that best describes the major pressure point of your child's grasp *most of the time*. Then look at your child's palm, and color in the block that best describes what your child's palm does most of the time.

Continue from left to right across the chart, coloring in one box per column according to the best description for your child. If your child uses a different grasp when she is holding different objects, use a blue crayon to show what she does with a block, and a green crayon to show what she does with cereal pieces. Or use any other colors that appeal to you.

After you have colored in the blocks, look at the colored blocks that go across the page, from left to right. Are all the blocks on one line colored in? If so, the type of grasp your child has is indicated in the *left* column, on the same line.

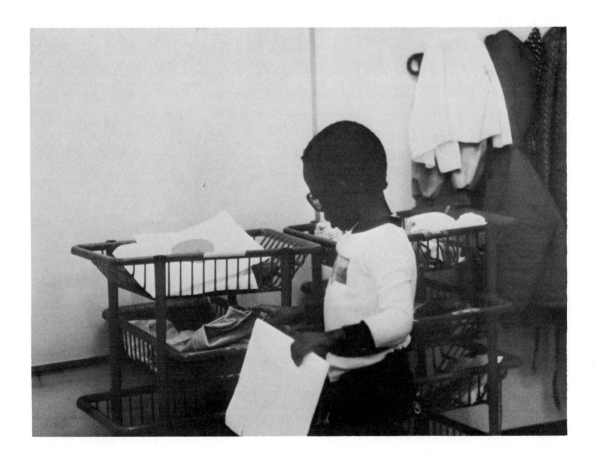

	Strength	Palm	Fingers	Index Finger	Thumb	Wrist
Your child's grasp is *reflexive* if:	Strength, pressure or holding point is in fingers, with no control by child, and	when palm is touched, fingers close automatically.				
Your child's grasp is *raking* if:	Strength, pressure or holding point is greatest in fingers farthest from thumb, and	the palm is not used, and	the fingers close against each other, and	the index finger is not separated from other fingers, and	the thumb is not used.	
Your child's grasp is *palmar* if:	Strength, pressure or holding point is greater in fingers toward thumb, and	the fingers squeeze against the palm, instead of against each other, and				
Your child's grasp is *whole-hand* if:	Strength, pressure or holding point is in index finger; fingers push against palm, and	the palm surrounds object; and	the fingers close toward palm, and	the index finger is more involved, and	the thumb is used slightly and pushes against object or fingers.	
Your child's grasp is *scissors* if:	Strength, pressure or holding point is between sides of thumb and index finger, and	(the palm is not necessarily used, and)	(the fingers may curve or not; not really involved in holding, and)	the side of the index finger closest to the thumb is used, and	the side of the thumb closest to the index finger is used.	
Your child's grasp is *forefinger* if:	Strength, pressure or holding point is between thumb tip and the under or palm side of index finger, and			the under or palm side of the index finger is used, and	the tip, or thumb pad is used.	
Your child's grasp is *pincer #1* if:	Strength, pressure or holding point is between thumb and index finger tips, and			the tip of the index finger is used, and	the tip or thumb pad is used, and	the wrist rests on surface.
Your child's grasp is *pincer #2* if:						the wrist does not need support.

Turn to page 128 in the HANDBOOK

Chapter 4. PICKING UP
Picking Up on Your Child's Reaching

Today's date _____
Your child's
age today _____

Many children show a *readiness* for reaching before they are actually able to reach toward and pick up something. Some of these prereaching behaviors are listed below.

If your child is not yet reaching, check any behaviors on this list you have seen your child do:

☐ Turns head toward sounds

☐ Follows objects with eyes

☐ Opens and closes hand if you show a favorite toy, or bottle, or makes a sound with a favorite toy

☐ Pats toys, table top, or highchair tray

☐ Searches for an object or toy that was dropped (may or may not find it!)

☐ Watches (almost stares) at own hand

☐ Plays with feet when lying on back

☐ Swipes at objects

☐ Looks back and forth from hands to nearby objects

☐ "Concentrates" when he hears a toy he likes

Are there any other things that your child does that make you think that he is getting ready to reach? What are they?

_____

_____

_____

If your child is *already* reaching, what is his reach like?

☐ Gets what he reaches for every time he tries

☐ Tries reaching, but doesn't always get what he wants because he:

☐ Sometimes can't grasp or hold on to the object

☐ Sometimes doesn't reach far enough

☐ Sometimes reaches too far; tries to grasp the object as if it were located further away than it really is

☐ Sometimes reaches and tries to grasp too far to the

　　☐ Right, or

　　☐ Left

If your child *tries* reaching, but doesn't always succeed, try to figure out *when* it happens, and *why*. Some reasons for over-reaching and under-reaching could be things like:

Shadows covering the object, or making it appear to be in a different place

Too much light in back of the object, so that it is difficult to see, or makes your child squint

Your child may not be able to see in certain parts of the eye (this is called either a field loss or a central loss, depending on where it is)

Your child may not be using one of his eyes (this is called amblyopia)

There is not enough light in the room

Your child has poor motor control

There could be other reasons, too. If your child is having difficulties with reaching, what do you think might be the reason?

_____

_____

_____

Turn to page 132 in the HANDBOOK ➤

Chapter 4. PICKING UP
Assessment of Voluntary Release

Today's date _____
Your child's
age today _____

The lists of behaviors below describe how children release objects from their hands. Check off in columns A, B, and C those that your child is able to do.

Column A

☐ Holds rattle for a few seconds then drops

☐ Flings or throws objects placed in hand

☐ Does not seem to know something is in hand

Column B

☐ Transfers object from one hand to the other

☐ Bangs objects together

☐ Drops things and searches for them

Column C

☐ Puts items in container

☐ Gives food or toy to someone else on request

☐ Stacks blocks

☐ Puts pegs in pegboard

☐ Puts puzzle together

Columns A, B, and C each correspond to a different stage in the development of release. Column A behaviors are undifferentiated — the child is really not aware of her hands and how she can use them. Colmn B behaviors show that the child is beginning to be aware of her hands and how she can manipulate objects. Column C behaviors indicate that the child understands objects and has mastered voluntary release.

Based on the behaviors you checked in the three columns, do you think your child has a voluntary release?

☐ Yes
☐ No, not yet

Why or why not?

_____

_____

_____

_____

Turn to page 133 in the HANDBOOK

Chapter 4. PICKING UP
Assessment of Wrist Rotation

Today's date _____
Your child's
age today _____

To see if your child has developed wrist rotation, check those skills
on the lists below that he is doing now:

☐ Picks up cup from table, takes a
drink, and then gives you the cup

☐ Picks up cup, drinks, and then drops
cup

☐ Spills food before spoon reaches
mouth

☐ Does not pick up cup, but puts
mouth on cup as it sits on table, and
tries to drink from cup that way

☐ Scoops and eats with spoon without
spilling

☐ Unscrews lids on jars

☐ Picks up cup, drinks, and returns to
table

☐ Gets peanut butter out of jar with knife

☐ Turns doorknobs

☐ Buttons shirt

If *most* of your checks are in the right column, chances are your
child has already learned wrist rotation, If *most* of the checks are in
the left column, your child is probably still working on it.

Turn to page 134 in the HANDBOOK →

Chapter 4. PICKING UP
Fine Motor Progress Chart

Movements	Date Assessed	Yes Child Does	Child Does Not Do Yet	Date Began To Work On	Date Child Does With Help	Child Does Alone
WEIGHT-BEARING: Takes weight on hands						
Takes weight on hands and arms (arms straight, palms flat)						
Takes weight on one hand and reaches: with the other						
with elbow bent						
with arm straight						
TYPES OF GRASPS: Reflexive						
Raking						
Palmar						
Whole-hand						
Scissors						
Forefinger						
Pincer						
REACHING: Seems to anticipate						
Swipes at objects						
Reaches to sound presented *at* ear level on side						
Reaches to sound presented *below* ear level on side						
Reaches to sound presented *above* ear level on side						

Movements	Date Assessed	Yes Child Does	Child Does Not Do Yet	Date Began To Work On	Date Child Does With Help	Child Does Alone
Reaches to sound presented in front						
Reaches and secures object						
VOLUNTARY RELEASE: Flings object						
Hands object to you						
Deliberately releases						
WRIST ROTATION: Turns wrist forward away from body						
Turns wrist backward toward body						
Turns wrist forward and back again						
READINESS: Scribbles with crayon						
Uses adult grasp of crayon or pencil						
Marks up and down: Repeatedly						
Once						
Marks left and right (horizontally): Repeatedly						
Once						
Marks circles: Repeatedly						
Once						
Marks cross (+)						

Turn to page 141 in the HANDBOOK

Chapter 5

COMING ACROSS:

Daily Living and Communicating

Today's date _____
Your child's
age today _____

Getting Ready

What is the natural setting for teaching the following self-care
skills? The first one has been done for you.

Brushing teeth *BATH ROOM* _____

Brushing hair _____

Toilet training _____

Eating _____

What are the naturally occurring times for these activities? You can
name more than one:

Brushing teeth_____

_____

Brushing hair _____

_____

Toilet training_____

_____

Eating _____

_____

Turn to page 146 in the HANDBOOK

Chapter 5. COMING ACROSS
Getting Ready, continued

Today's date _____
Your child's
age today _____

Listed below are several steps involved in washing your hands. Put them in order, first to last, by placing a number in the space before each step.

____ Rinses soap off
____ Turns on water
____ Locates sink and faucets
____ Puts soap in or on soapdish
____ Dries hands with towel
____ Locates towel
____ Locates soap
____ Wets hands
____ Lathers hands, front and back
____ Turns off water
____ Hangs up towel

You are planning to teach your child how to take off a pullover shirt. First, take your own pullover shirt off slowly, analyzing the steps you go through to take it completely off. Then, write the steps in order below:

1. _____
2. _____
3. _____
4. _____
5. _____
6. _____
7. _____
8. _____
9. _____
10. _____

11. _____
12. _____
13. _____
14. _____
15. _____
16. _____
17. _____
18. _____
19. _____
20. _____

Turn to page 147 in the HANDBOOK

Chapter 5. COMING ACROSS
Getting Ready, continued

Today's date _____
Your child's
age today _____

Use the space below to describe your typical day. List *what* you did,
who you did it with, *how long* it took, etc.

5:00–6:00 A.M.

What _____

With whom _____

How long _____

6:00–7:00 A.M.

What _____

With whom _____

How long _____

7:00–8:00 A.M.

What _____

With whom _____

How long _____

8:00–9:00 A.M.

What _____

With whom _____

How long _____

9:00–10:00 A.M.

What _____

With whom _____

How long _____

10:00–11:00 A.M.

What _____

With whom _____

How long _____

11:00–12:00 Noon

What _____

With whom _____

How long _____

Getting Ready

12:00–1:00 P.M.

What _____

With whom_____

How long _____

1:00–2:00 P.M.

What _____

With whom_____

How long _____

2:00–3:00 P.M.

What _____

With whom_____

How long _____

3:00–4:00 P.M.

What _____

With whom_____

How long _____

4:00–5:00 P.M.

What _____

With whom_____

How long _____

5:00–6:00 P.M.

What _____

With whom_____

How long _____

6:00–7:00 P.M.

What _____

With whom_____

How long _____

7:00–8:00 P.M.

What _____

With whom_____

How long _____

8:00–9:00 P.M.

What _____

With whom_____

How long _____

9:00–10:00 P.M.

What _____

With whom _____

How long _____

10:00–11:00 P.M.

What _____

With whom _____

How long _____

11:00–12:00 Midnight

What _____

With whom _____

How long _____

After looking at your day, where are the problem areas?

_____

_____

_____

_____

Do these problem areas concern your visually or multiply handicapped child? In other words, is the problem *caused* by your child,
or is it just a problem area in general?

_____

_____

_____

_____

If your visually or multiply handicapped child does cause the
problem, is there something you can do to change the situation,
change your child's behavior, change what you are asking your
child to do, or change the time of day when you do it? Please
describe what you might do:

_____

_____

_____

_____

Turn to page 147 in the HANDBOOK ➡

Chapter 5. COMING ACROSS
Eating Skills

Today's date _____
Your child's
age today _____

In the spaces on the left below, list your child's favorite foods. Then check off on the right whether those foods are soft, mushy, chewy, or hard.

	Soft	Mushy	Chewy	Hard
_____	☐	☐	☐	☐
_____	☐	☐	☐	☐
_____	☐	☐	☐	☐
_____	☐	☐	☐	☐
_____	☐	☐	☐	☐
_____	☐	☐	☐	☐
_____	☐	☐	☐	☐
_____	☐	☐	☐	☐
_____	☐	☐	☐	☐
_____	☐	☐	☐	☐

Does your child only eat one texture?

☐ Yes   ☐ No

If yes, which texture?_____

What are your child's *least* favorite foods? List them below in the spaces on the left, and then check off whether those foods are soft, mushy, chewy, or hard.

	Soft	Mushy	Chewy	Hard
_____	☐	☐	☐	☐
_____	☐	☐	☐	☐
_____	☐	☐	☐	☐
_____	☐	☐	☐	☐
_____	☐	☐	☐	☐
_____	☐	☐	☐	☐
_____	☐	☐	☐	☐
_____	☐	☐	☐	☐
_____	☐	☐	☐	☐
_____	☐	☐	☐	☐

Check off any of the methods you have used to get your child to eat these foods:

☐ Covering with favorite food (for example, spinach covered by applesauce)

☐ Blending to a softer consistency

☐ Cooking in a different way (cooking carrots with brown sugar, for example)

☐ Offering food your child likes if he will eat the food he doesn't like

☐ Saying something like, "Daddy loves spinach. Let's take a bite for daddy. Show daddy what a big girl you are."

☐ Having your child help you prepare the food

Turn to page 150 in the HANDBOOK ➤

Chapter 5. COMING ACROSS
Eating Skills, continued

Today's date _____
Your child's
age today _____

Teach someone how to use a spoon to eat cold cereal from a bowl,
using the follwing steps:

1. First, *sit in front* of that person

2. Now, put your hand on the other person's hand and move them through the
following steps:

   a. Put your hand on his
   b. Pick up the spoon
   c. Scoop up some cereal from the bowl
   d. Take the spoon to his mouth

3. Now, *sit behind* the person, and repeat the same steps

Which position felt more comfortable for you?
☐ In front
☐ Behind
Which position gave you the most information about how the
person you taught was doing?
☐ In front
☐ Behind
Which position felt the most comfortable for the person you
taught?
☐ In front
☐ Behind
Which position gave the person you taught the most
information?
☐ In front
☐ Behind

Turn to page 152 in the HANDBOOK

Chapter 5. COMING ACROSS
Toilet Training

Today's date _____
Your child's
age today _____

If your child is not toilet trained yet, or you are just beginning the process of toilet training, keep a chart for two weeks that indicates when your child eliminates.

Hang the chart on the next page in the bathroom where you can get to it easily. Check your child every half-hour.

Use the symbols below to record on the chart what you find when you check your child:

In toilet: Urine = V
Bowel movement = *BM*
Urine and bowel movemnt = *UBM*

In pants: Urine = (*V*)
Bowel movement = (*BM*)
Urine and bowel movement = (*UBM*)

Toilet Training

TOILET TRAINING CHART

Date

Time															
7:00 A.M.															
7:30															
8:00															
8:30															
9:00															
9:30															
10:00															
10:30															
11:00															
11:30															
12:00 Noon															
12:30 P.M.															
1:00															
1:30															
2:00															
2:30															
3:00															
3:30															
4:00															
4:30															
5:00															
5:30															
6:00															
6:30															
7:00															
7:30															
8:00															
8:30															
9:00 P.M															

After two weeks, look at the chart and decide what your child's schedule is. When does he usually urinate? When do his bowel movements normally occur?

For example, look at the sample chart below. Use that chart to answer the follwing questions:

This child has a bowel movement between _____ and _____.

This child usually urinates in the early morning between _____ and _____.

This child should be taken to the toilet at _____ and checked every 15 minutes so that he will have success in the toilet.

What is the best time to potty this child around lunchtime? _____

What is the best time to potty this child around suppertime? _____

TOILET TRAINING CHART

Time	2/26	2/27	2/28	3/1	3/2	3/3	3/4	3/5	3/6	3/7	3/8	3/9	3/10	3/11
7:00 A.M.						(U)					U	U	(U)	U
7:30			(U)		(U)		(U)	(U)	(U)	(U)				
8:00														
8:30														
9:00														
9:30		(BM)					(BM)					(BM)		
10:00														
10:30				(BM)						(BM)				
11:00														
11:30	U						(U)		U					
12:00 Noon		U	(U)		(UBM)	(U)				U	U		U	U
12:30 P.M.				U				(U)						
1:00												(U)		
1:30														
2:00														
2:30														
3:00														
3:30														
4:00	(U)													
4:30		(U)		(U)										
5:00			(U)		(U)			(U)	(UBM)				U	
5:30	(BM)						(U)			(U)	U	U		(U)
6:00						(U)								
6:30														
7:00														
7:30														
8:00														
8:30														
9:00 P.M														

Toilet Training

Here are some extra toileting charts for your use. You may find that your child is not yet ready for toilet training, and you will want to wait a while and mark the charts again at a later time.

TOILET TRAINING CHART

Date

Time													
7:00 A.M.													
7:30													
8:00													
8:30													
9:00													
9:30													
10:00													
10:30													
11:00													
11:30													
12:00 Noon													
12:30 P.M.													
1:00													
1:30													
2:00													
2:30													
3:00													
3:30													
4:00													
4:30													
5:00													
5:30													
6:00													
6:30													
7:00													
7:30													
8:00													
8:30													
9:00 P.M													

TOILET TRAINING CHART

Time							Date							
7:00 A.M.														
7:30														
8:00														
8:30														
9:00														
9:30														
10:00														
10:30														
11:00														
11:30														
12:00 Noon														
12:30 P.M.														
1:00														
1:30														
2:00														
2:30														
3:00														
3:30														
4:00														
4:30														
5:00														
5:30														
6:00														
6:30														
7:00														
7:30														
8:00														
8:30														
9:00 P.M														

Toilet Training

TOILET TRAINING CHART

Date

Time														
7:00 A.M.														
7:30														
8:00														
8:30														
9:00														
9:30														
10:00														
10:30														
11:00														
11:30														
12:00 Noon														
12:30 P.M.														
1:00														
1:30														
2:00														
2:30														
3:00														
3:30														
4:00														
4:30														
5:00														
5:30														
6:00														
6:30														
7:00														
7:30														
8:00														
8:30														
9:00 P.M														

Turn to page 157 in the HANDBOOK

Chapter 5. COMING ACROSS
Learning to Communicate

Today's date _____
Your child's
age today _____

At what stage of language development is your child?

Expressive
- ☐ Crying
- ☐ Cooing
- ☐ Turn-talking
- ☐ Babbling
- ☐ Imitation of sounds
- ☐ Imitation of words
- ☐ Use of words in meaningful way
- ☐ Use of phrases
- ☐ Use of sentences
- ☐ Good language with some speech problems
- ☐ Good language with no problems

Receptive
- ☐ Quiets when talked to
- ☐ Listens
- ☐ Takes turns
- ☐ Gestures
- ☐ Points
- ☐ Understands concepts
- ☐ Follows one-step command
- ☐ Follows complicated command
- ☐ Has complete understanding of concepts

Turn to page 159 in the HANDBOOK →

Chapter 5. COMING ACROSS
First Communications

Today's date _____
Your child's
age today _____

Make a tape recording of your verbal interaction with your child. If a tape recording is not possible, then ask another adult to observe you and your child and write down everything that you say to your child, and that your child says to you. Do this for 15 minutes.

Your friend can use this page to write down what was said. Or, if you were able to make a tape recording, listen to it now, and use this page to write down what you heard.

How long were you and your child able to interact?

☐ All 15 minutes
☐ Less than 15 minutes (how long? _____)

What kinds of things did you say to your child? Depending on your child's stage of communication, you could have said nonsense words, used cooing voice, imitated your child, asked questions, told her to do something, etc. Describe your language in the space below:

_____

_____

_____

_____

_____

What tone of voice did you use?

☐ High pitched   ☐ Soft
☐ Low pitched   ☐ Loud
☐ Silly
☐ Matter of fact

How long did your child communicate with you?

☐ All 15 minutes
☐ Less than 15 minutes (how long? _____)

Was there any turn-talking? If so, give an example in the space below:

_____

_____

_____

Was there active listening on both *your* part and *your child*'s part?

_____

_____

_____

Turn to page 161 in the HANDBOOK ➤

Chapter 5. COMING ACROSS
The Second Stage: Imitation

Today's date _____
Your child's
age today _____

Which of the following lets you know that your child understands
what is being communicated:

☐ You can jingle your car keys and your child heads for the
closet to get his coat.

☐ Your child sits on the kitchen floor and points to the
refrigerator door.

☐ Your child continues to play with the oven door after you
say, "No!"

☐ You say to your child, "Come, Johnny," and he raises his
hands and arms toward you.

Make a list in the space below of three things that your child does
that let you know that he understands what it is you are saying:

1. _____

2. _____

3. _____

Turn to page 163 in the HANDBOOK

Chapter 5. COMING ACROSS
The Second Stage: Imitation, continued

Today's date _____
Your child's
age today _____

Play a game with your child:

Place two objects in front of your child. Let him feel them and/or look at them very carefully.

Take them out of his hands, place them back on the table, and say, "Show me the _____."

Teach your child that the way you want him to show you is by pointing to the object that you named. Your child may have to touch the object to point to it, but eventually he may be able to point to it without touching.

Play this game in various rooms in the house. Give an example of how you would play this game in each of the following places (that is, what objects would you use?):

Bathtub _____

Kitchen table_____

Coat closet _____

Turn to page 164 in the HANDBOOK

Chapter 5. COMING ACROSS
The Third Stage: Expanding Vocabulary

Today's date _____
Your child's
age today _____

How do you feel about saying, "No!" to your visually or multiply handicapped child?

_____

_____

_____

_____

Are you consistent about the times when you say "No"? For instance, do you say, "Please don't touch my glasses," but then let him wear your glasses and play with them as if they were sunglasses?

_____

List the times or kinds of situations in which you say "No" to your child:

1. _____
2. _____
3. _____
4. _____
5. _____
6. _____
7. _____

◄ **Turn to page 165 in the HANDBOOK**

Chapter 5. COMING ACROSS
Expanding Vocabulary, continued

Today's date _____
Your child's
age today _____

Visit your public library and have the librarian help you make up a list of nursery rhymes and books appropriate for your child's age.

Teach your child the nursery rhymes and songs that have some meaning for her. Also teach her some of the nonsense rhymes and riddles, as they are good for listening, rhythm, and imitation.

List some of the books you found here:

_____
_____
_____
_____
_____
_____
_____
_____
_____
_____

Register your child with the Library of Congress so that he can receive the Talking Book Service. The service provides a special tape recorder or record player and will send records to your child that you request.

The address of the Library of Congress is:

National Library Service for the
  Blind and Physically Handicapped
Library of Congress
1291 Taylor Street, N.W.
Washington, D.C. 20542

(202) 707-5100

To find out which library in your state is responsible for the Talking Book Service, you may also write to:

National Consultant in Early Childhood
American Foundation for the Blind
15 West 16th Street
New York, NY 10001

Turn to page 166 in the HANDBOOK →

Chapter 5. COMING ACROSS
Expanding Vocabulary, continued

Today's date _____
Your child's
age today _____

Make a list in the space below of the words that your child uses
consistently. Add to this list as your child learns new words.

1. _____   7. _____
2. _____   8. _____
3. _____   9. _____
4. _____   10. _____
5. _____   11. _____
6. _____   12. _____

Does your child know the important words in his environment?
Check the ones he can identify:

☐ Bed   ☐ Bathroom
☐ Toybox   ☐ Clock
☐ Kitchen   ☐ Living room
☐ Garage   ☐ Playroom
☐ Back yard   ☐ Front yard
☐ Driveway   ☐ Bush
☐ Sidewalk   ☐ Mailbox
☐ Sofa   ☐ Table
☐ Front door   ☐ Swing set

Others: _____

_____
_____
_____

Turn to page 167 in the HANDBOOK

THINKING IT THROUGH:

Knowing Oneself and Understanding the World

Today's date _____
Your child's
age today _____

Sensory Development

Choose three experiences you had today from those listed below,
and describe the sensory information you received from each.

For example, if you had a shower today, your sensory experiences
would be:

Touch (warm water)
Smell (soap)
Hearing (sound of water running)
Vision (looking for face cloth)
Taste (water running down your face into your mouth)

Eating breakfast:_____

_____

_____

Grocery shopping: _____

_____

_____

Driving car:_____

_____

_____

Preparing a meal: _____

_____

_____

Chapter 6. THINKING IT THROUGH
Sensory Development

At exercise class: _____
_____
_____
_____

At playground or park: _____
_____
_____
_____

Other: _____
_____
_____
_____

Which of your senses gives you the *most* information? _____
_____

Turn to page 175 in the HANDBOOK

Today's date _____
Your child's
age today _____

Chapter 6. THINKING IT THROUGH
Smell and Taste

The next time you go to a shopping mall, pay attention to the various odors. In some cases, you will be able to identify a type of store without even walking into it. If your child is with you, be sure to identify the odors and talk about what each one means. If possible, make the experience meaningful for your child. For example, if you smell pizza, buy a slice to share with your child!

Check out the smells in your shopping mall:

☐ Pizza   ☐ Cinnamon buns
☐ Chocolate chip cookies   ☐ Leather
☐ Flowers   ☐ Candles
☐ Trash cans   ☐ Soaps
☐ Hamburgers   ☐ French fries
☐ Wood/furniture   ☐ Others: _____

If you live in the city, odors are a bit harder to identify because they are so unpredictable and seem to come from everywhere—and often come all at the same time. Try to identify the odors coming from each of the locations listed below. Some examples are given.

Street corner: car exhaust; _____

Bakery: bread; _____

Newsstand: newsprint; _____

Grocery: laundry detergent; _____

Fruit stand: flowers; _____

Delicatessen: pickles; _____

Bar: popcorn; _____

Hot dog stand: sauerkraut; _____

Gymnasium: perspiration; _____

If you live in the country, you will notice many distinctive odors, some of which will depend on the time of year. Try to identify the smells associated with the following seasons. Some examples are given.

Spring: newly-turned earth; _____

Summer: fertilizer; _____

Fall: harvested grain; _____

Winter: wood-burning fires; _____

Chapter 6. THINKING IT THROUGH
Smell and Taste

What are the typical smells in your home that your visually or
multiply handicapped child uses to identify what is happening?
(Add to the list if you want.)

- ☐ Eggs cooking
- ☐ Powder in bathroom after showering
- ☐ Soup cooking
- ☐ Your perfume or aftershave lotion
- ☐ Nail polish
- ☐ Heater
- ☐ Car exhaust

- ☐ Other_____

Turn to page 176 in the HANDBOOK

Chapter 6. THINKING IT THROUGH
Smell and Taste, continued

Today's date _____
Your child's
age today _____

Expose your child to many tastes. For his lunch, plan a menu that
will include all different kinds of tastes by circling an item in each
category, or adding a food of your own:

    Sour: pickles, vinegar, plain yogurt, _____
    Sweet: fruit yogurt, fruit, cake, cookies, _____
    Salt: potato chips, pretzels, crackers _____
    Tart: apples, lemonade, _____
    Bland: oatmeal, mashed potatoes, grits, _____
    Spicy: chili, tacos, _____

Talk about the foods your child eats and have him tell you how they
taste.

Turn to page 177 in the HANDBOOK

Chapter 6. THINKING IT THROUGH
Touch

Today's date _____
Your child's
age today _____

What does your child like to touch?

☐ Soft things   ☐ Rough things
☐ People   ☐ Toys
☐ Fuzzy things   ☐ Food
☐ Slippery things   ☐ Mushy things

Are there some substances that your child will not touch?   ☐ Yes
                                                              ☐ No

If yes, what are they?_____

_____

_____

_____

_____

Will he touch things today that he absolutely refused to touch
when he was younger?   ☐ Yes
                         ☐ No

How does your child touch things?

☐ Just his finger   ☐ Brings to mouth
☐ Whole hand   ☐ Sticks out tongue
☐ Rubs object on his body ☐ Uses two hands

☐ Other: _____

_____

Keep a box by your child's favorite place to be in the daytime. Keep
different feeling objects in this box so that you and your child can
play with them during the day. Continue to introduce your child to
new and different textures, even if at first he is hesitant about
touching them.

Turn to page 179 in the HANDBOOK

Chapter 6. THINKING IT THROUGH
Vision

Today's date _____
Your child's
age today _____

What is your child's eye condition?

_____

_____

Which of these does she see?
- ☐ Light
- ☐ Shadows
- ☐ People
- ☐ Large toys
- ☐ Small toys

- ☐ Animals
- ☐ Food
- ☐ Bottle
- ☐ Patterns
- ☐ Other (please describe)

_____

_____

_____

Indicate what she sees:

All of the time _____

Some of the time _____

Only once in a while _____

What does your child do to let you know that she sees?
- ☐ Changes position of body
- ☐ Stops moving and looks
- ☐ Holds head still
- ☐ Follows with eyes
- ☐ Rocks back and forth
- ☐ Reaches out
- ☐ Asks a question
- ☐ Holds things close to one eye
- ☐ Holds things close to both eyes
- ☐ Turns head in funny way

- ☐ Other _____

Turn to page 180 in the HANDBOOK ➡

Chapter 6. THINKING IT THROUGH
The Visual Response Continuum

Today's date _____
Your child's
age today _____

Turn on the ceiling light in a dark room. What does your child do?

_____

_____

Hold a penlight or a small disposable flashlight covered with colored cellophane about 12 inches from your child's face. Shine the light to the bridge of the nose. Check off everything that your child does in response:

☐ Closes eyes
☐ Seems to focus on the light
☐ Turns away
☐ Does not respond

☐ Other: _____

_____

_____

Move the light slowly to the left, stop, and then move it back again past the nose to the right, and stop again. Check your child's response:

☐ Follows light with head and eyes
☐ Follows light with eyes only
☐ Seems to focus when light stops
☐ Focuses once light moves past nose
☐ Does not respond

☐ Other: _____

_____

_____

This time, start with the light shining on your child's right ear, and then move it around in front of your child's eyes until it shines on the left ear. Check your child's response:

☐ Eyes move to focus on light before it reaches the nose
☐ Head turns to light as soon as it begins to move:
    ☐ Head turns to right side
    ☐ Head turns to left side
    ☐ Head turns first to one side, then the other

☐ Follows light all the way
☐ Loses light, cannot follow it:
    ☐ On right side
    ☐ In middle of body
    ☐ On left side

☐ Follows light smoothly
☐ Follows light in a jerky fashion

Now repeat the first three steps, but use your face instead of a flashlight. Stay about 9 to 12 inches away from your child's face, and try not to talk. Does your child respond:

☐ The same way as when you used the light?
☐ By seeming to focus on your face, but not really following with interest unless you talk to her?

☐ Other: _____

_____

_____

Repeat the first three steps again, but use one of your child's favorite toys. What happens?

☐ Child responds the same way he did to lights
☐ Child responds the same way he did to your face
☐ Child responds only if the toy makes a sound
☐ Child does not appear interested

☐ Other: _____

_____

_____

How does your child respond to strangers?

☐ Does not realize person is a stranger
☐ Cries or appears frightened
☐ Looks at stranger, smiles, and talks
☐ Politely, but carefully

☐ Other: _____

_____

_____

Does your child know the different between:

	Yes	No
Mommy and daddy	☐	☐
You and another relative	☐	☐
You and a visitor	☐	☐
A real shoe and a picture of a shoe	☐	☐

How do you know that your child knows the difference?
What does your child do?

_____

_____

_____

Chapter 6. THINKING IT THROUGH
The Visual Response Continuum

Does your child have to have sound or voice cues before he can tell
the difference between you and other people?   ☐ Usually
                                                ☐ Sometimes
                                                ☐ Never

Using a penlight or small flashlight again, move the light farther
and farther away from your child.
    How far away are you when he no longer seems to pay attention?

Turn out the room lights so the room is partially dark. Try
moving the light again. Now, how far can you move the light
before your child does not pay attention any more?

Does your child see things   ☐ Near to him?
                              ☐ Far from him?

Turn to page 183 in the **HANDBOOK**

Chapter 6. THINKING IT THROUGH
The Visual Response Continuum, continued

Today's date _____
Your child's
age today _____

Observe which of the following skills your child demonstrates and then think of an activity you might use to reinforce these. For example, if your child matches objects, pictures, and symbols, your child could help you sort laundry. If he has some vision, your child could sort by color and size. If his vision is severely limited, he can still pull out all the socks for the underwear load.

Skill: Shows fixation

Home activity: _____

Skill: Looks at simple patterns

Home activity: _____

Skill: Looks at small objects

Home activity: _____

Skill: Looks at hand

Home activity: _____

Skill: Looks at face

Home activity: _____

Skill: Sees small objects near him and far away

Home activity: _____

Skill: Sees large objects

Home activity: _____

Skill: Begins puzzles

Home activity: _____

Skill: Matches objects, pictures, and symbols

Home activity: _____

The Visual Response Continuum

For each of the activities listed below, indicate what skill or skills
are required.

T = Tracking
F = Focusing
M = Crossing midline
R = Reaching
P = Placing objects in something

_____ Following balloon as it moves across the crib
_____ Putting clothespins in bag
_____ Looking at mommy's face
_____ Moving stuffed toy from right hand to left hand
_____ Picking up cup
_____ Putting away toys

Turn to page 184 in the HANDBOOK

Chapter 6. THINKING IT THROUGH

Hearing

Today's date _____
Your child's
age today _____

What does your child do to show you that he hears?

☐ Stops crying, quiets
☐ Tilts head
☐ Makes babbling noises
☐ Turns his head
☐ Reaches out for sound source
☐ Carries out verbal direction
☐ Talks
☐ Answers questions

How near to him does the noise have to be in order for him to hear it?

☐ 3 inches
☐ 6 inches
☐ 1 foot
☐ 2 feet
☐ 6 feet

Which sounds does your child prefer?

☐ Vacuum
☐ Rattle
☐ Bell
☐ Soft music
☐ Loud music

☐ Talking
☐ Washing machine
☐ Television
☐ Makes no difference

☐ Others: _____

Turn to page 190 in the HANDBOOK →

Chapter 6. THINKING IT THROUGH
Hearing, continued

Today's date _____
Your child's
age today _____

Play a guessing game with your child. Use a variety of objects that make noise in your child's everyday life. Have him guess, "What made the sound."

Write the date at the top of the column. Each time you play the game with your child throughout the day, mark the chart
   Y = Yes
   N = No
to keep track of your child's success.

Add to your list any other sounds that are important in your home.

Sounds	Date								
Alarm clock									
Vacuum cleaner									
Ticking clock									
Radiator coming on									
Roar of fire (stove fireplace, or gas burner)									
Car									
Telephone									
Dog moving									
Dog barking									
Other:									

Turn to page 193 in the HANDBOOK ➤

Chapter 6. THINKING IT THROUGH
Body Awareness

Today's date _____
Your child's
age today _____

Which of the body parts below can your child point to when asked?
If she is unable to point, decide if she is trying to tell you in some
other way that she knows the answer (such as moving the body part
slightly, or looking at it).

☐ Eyes	☐ Head	☐ Elbow
☐ Nose	☐ Arm	☐ Leg
☐ Mouth	☐ Hand	☐ Foot
☐ Hair	☐ Thumb	☐ Knee
☐ Face	☐ Fingers	☐ Ankle
☐ Tummy	☐ Back	☐ Shoulder
☐ Neck	☐ Backside	☐ Chest
☐ Toes	☐ Ears	

Check off those body parts your child can find on you:

☐ Eyes	☐ Head	☐ Elbow
☐ Nose	☐ Arm	☐ Leg
☐ Mouth	☐ Hand	☐ Foot
☐ Hair	☐ Thumb	☐ Knee
☐ Face	☐ Fingers	☐ Ankle
☐ Tummy	☐ Back	☐ Shoulder
☐ Neck	☐ Backside	☐ Chest
☐ Toes	☐ Ears	

Now get a little more abstract — can your child show you that she
knows her:

☐ Sides?	☐ Back?
☐ Front?	☐ Top?
☐ Bottom?	

Turn to page 196 in the HANDBOOK

Chapter 6. THINKING IT THROUGH
Cognitive Development

Today's date _____
Your child's
age today _____

Make a list of furniture, objects, and "landmarks" in your child's room.

1. _____   6. _____   11. _____
2. _____   7. _____   12. _____
3. _____   8. _____   13. _____
4. _____   9. _____   14. _____
5. _____   10. _____   16. _____

Ask yourself some questions about your child's room.

	Yes	No
Is is light enough?	☐	☐
Can he reach things in his crib?	☐	☐
Is there a mirror in his crib?	☐	☐
Are there too many colors in his room?	☐	☐
Are there too many patterns in his room?	☐	☐
Can he reach his bureaus and closet to help get things and put them away?	☐	☐
Is the room safe to move about in?	☐	☐
Is there open space in the room for your child to play?	☐	☐
Is there a container in which to put toys away?	☐	☐

Turn to page 199 in the HANDBOOK

Chapter 6. THINKING IT THROUGH
Object Permanence

Today's date _____
Your child's
age today _____

Does your child:	Yes	No
Throw toys haphazardly?	☐	☐
Drop toys and wait for you to pick them up?	☐	☐
Try to find things he's dropped?	☐	☐
Cry when you leave the room?	☐	☐
Find a music box if you put it under a blanket?	☐	☐

Which of the behaviors below demonstrate object permanence?*
- ☐ 1. Smiling at sound of your voice when you are out of reach
- ☐ 2. Smiling at sound of someone else's voice
- ☐ 3. Reaching
- ☐ 4. Crawling
- ☐ 5. Turning head to sound
- ☐ 6. Asking for a drink
- ☐ 7. Pointing to your nose
- ☐ 8. Handing toy to brother or sister
- ☐ 9. Stacking blocks
- ☐ 10. Saying "Daddy work"

Do you think your child has object permanence?   ☐ Yes
                                                  ☐ Not yet

Why or why not?

_____

_____

_____

Turn to page 200 in the HANDBOOK

*Answers: 1, 6, 8, 10

Chapter 6. THINKING IT THROUGH
Object Constancy

Today's date _____
Your child's
age today _____

If your child has enough vision, does she get excited when she sees a familiar object that is out of her reach?

☐ Yes   ☐ No

If Yes, please give an example: _____

Which of these behaviors demonstrate object constancy?*
☐ 1. Child sees dog, and says "dog"
☐ 2. Child sees cat, and says "dog"
☐ 3. Child calls all men she sees "da-da"
☐ 4. Child will only drink from "her" cup
☐ 5. Child identifies trucks and cars by sound
☐ 6. Child matches objects by sight or touch

Does your child understand that there are different kinds of cups? That is, she says "cup" or puts a cup to her mouth, regardless of whether she is given a mug, glass, china cup, plastic cup, or toy cup?
☐ Yes
☐ Doesn't seem to; gives no visible sign

Does your child *over*generalize? That is, does she put *every* container to her mouth as if it were a cup?
☐ Yes
☐ Doesn't seem to; gives no visible sign

Is there some other example you could give to describe your child's knowledge or use of object constancy? For example, does she match and sort objects? Please describe:

_____
_____
_____
_____
_____

Turn to page 203 in the HANDBOOK →

*Answers: 1, 2, 3, 5, 6

Chapter 6. THINKING IT THROUGH
Knowing Oneself

Today's date _____
Your child's
age today _____

The behaviors listed below suggest that a child is beginning to realize that she is an individual who can have some control over the things and people around her.

Check those behaviors that you have observed in your child:
- ☐ Deliberately drops objects and waits for you to pick them up for her
- ☐ Turns when you call her name
- ☐ Cries when you leave the room
- ☐ Holds arms up to you to be picked up
- ☐ Uses words to make wants known ("milk," "cookie").

☐ Other: _____

Turn to page 205 in the HANDBOOK

Chapter 6. THINKING IT THROUGH
Cause and Effect

Today's date _____
Your child's
age today _____

Which of the following behaviors demonstrate cause and effect?
☐ Pulling on napkin to get cookie that is out of reach
☐ Hitting or batting at mechanical toy that has stopped moving
☐ Stacking objects
☐ Putting objects in containers and dumping them out again
☐ Climbing out of the crib
☐ Drinking from a bottle
☐ Drinking from a cup independently
☐ Crying when hungry

Does your child have a knowledge of cause-and-effect relationships?
☐ Usually
☐ Sometimes
☐ Not yet

Give reason for your answer: _____
_____
_____

Turn to page 208 in the HANDBOOK

Chapter 6. THINKING IT THROUGH
Categorization

Today's date _____
Your child's
age today _____

Items can be classified according to their *physical attributes,* the *group* to which they belong, their *function*, or their *association* with other things in the environment.

For each set of objects below, decide on what basis they were grouped together, and check the appropriate column:

	Attributes	Group	Function	Association
Cat, dog, bird, bear	☐	☐	☐	☐
Dog, cow, horse	☐	☐	☐	☐
Knife, fork, spoon	☐	☐	☐	☐
Cup, plate, spoon, bowl	☐	☐	☐	☐
Apple, pear, banana	☐	☐	☐	☐
Apple, cherry, tomato	☐	☐	☐	☐
All first-graders	☐	☐	☐	☐
Donut, ball, plate	☐	☐	☐	☐
Boots, umbrella, raincoat	☐	☐	☐	☐
Shirt, pants, jacket	☐	☐	☐	☐
Tent, sleeping bag, canteen	☐	☐	☐	☐
Chair, sofa, recliner	☐	☐	☐	☐
Cassette, record, radio	☐	☐	☐	☐
Paper, pencil, book	☐	☐	☐	☐
Doorway, bed, book	☐	☐	☐	☐

Turn to page 214 in the HANDBOOK ➡

LOOKING AHEAD:

The School Years and Beyond

Today's date _____
Your child's
age today _____

Advice from Parents

Contact parents of preschool, elementary, and junior/senior high school visually handicapped students through your local parent-teacher association, parent group, or national parent association.

Ask these parents about some of the difficulties their child faced in becoming independent. Be prepared to help your child over these stumbling blocks, or to avoid them altogether.

Name: _____

Address: _____

Phone: _____

Advice given: _____

_____

_____

Name: _____

Address: _____

Phone: _____

Advice given: _____

_____

_____

Name: _____

Address: _____

Phone: _____

Advice given: _____

_____

_____

Advice from Parents, continued

Name: _____

Address: _____

Phone: _____

Advice given: _____

_____

_____

Name: _____

Address: _____

Phone: _____

Advice given: _____

_____

_____

Name: _____

Address: _____

Phone: _____

Advice given: _____

_____

_____

Name: _____

Address: _____

Phone: _____

Advice given: _____

_____

_____

Name: _____

Address: _____

Phone: _____

Advice given: _____

_____

_____

Name: _____

Address: _____

Phone: _____

Advice given: _____

_____

Name: _____

Address: _____

Phone: _____

Advice given: _____

_____

Name: _____

Address: _____

Phone: _____

Advice given: _____

_____

Name: _____

Address: _____

Phone: _____

Advice given: _____

_____

Name: _____

Address: _____

Phone: _____

Advice given: _____

_____

Turn to page 222 in the HANDBOOK →

Chapter 7. LOOKING AHEAD
Independence Training

Today's date _____
Your child's
age today _____

Check off some of the "finer points" in the self-care, body image, and problem-solving areas that you feel are important for your child to be able to do so that he acts and looks like any other child or young adult.

Add your own:

☐ Dresses self   _____

☐ Chooses own clothing   _____

☐ Feeds self   _____

☐ Uses knife and fork   _____

☐ Drinks with a straw   _____

☐ Combs hair   _____

☐ Cleans fingernails   _____

☐ Washes face   _____

☐ Has good posture   _____

☐ Chooses own meals at restaurants   _____

☐ Makes meals at home   _____

☐ Walks to school without you   _____

☐ Goes shopping without you   _____

☐ Asks directions   _____

☐ Uses telephone   _____

Keep these points in mind when you are working with your child in these areas!

← Turn to page 225 in the HANDBOOK

Chapter 7. LOOKING AHEAD
Finding an Advocate

Find someone in your community—a friend, a relative, or a professional—to be an advocate for you. Choose someone who will be available to you and will help you fight for your child's rights.

You can find an advocate by looking in the yellow or white pages under "Protection and Advocacy" or "Developmental Disabilities" or "Handicapped Law Project." Check also with a nearby law school — call the dean's office and ask if the school has a clinical program where law students can assist in local cases.

Your advocate's name:

_____

Telephone number:

_____

You will also find that others can sometimes become an advocate for you when you have a problem.

Make your problems known to:

Clergy
Congressional representatives
State legislators
Mayor of your town
Your city council
Newspaper editors

Turn to page 228 in the HANDBOOK →

Chapter 7. LOOKING AHEAD
Your Child's Educational Rights

Today's date _____
Your child's
age today _____

Regardless of your child's age, you can use this checklist to determine if the public school or early childhood program is following the basic ideas behind the Education for All Handicapped Children Act. They only apply, however, if your child is between the ages of 3 and 21 years, and if your state requires that a child of that age should be in school.

Place a check mark in the column that best answers the following questions:

Evaluation

Date of Evaluation: _____

	Yes	No	Not Sure
1. Did you receive a written notice that your child was going to be evaluated?	☐	☐	☐
Did it tell you why the school wanted to evaluate your child?	☐	☐	☐
Did it tell you what tests would be used?	☐	☐	☐
Did it tell you when your child would be evaluated?	☐	☐	☐
2. Were you asked to sign a paper that gave the school your permission to evaluate?	☐	☐	☐
3. Did you receive a copy of the evaluation report?	☐	☐	☐
4. Was more than one test used?	☐	☐	☐
5. Were the tests valid for use with your child?	☐	☐	☐
6. Were the people who gave the tests qualified?	☐	☐	☐
7. Were the people who gave the tests experienced in the area of blindness and visual impairment?	☐	☐	☐
If not, did someone who understands visual handicaps interpret the test results?	☐	☐	☐

Your Child's Educational Rights

	Yes	No	Not Sure
Individual Educational Program (IEP)			
Date of IEP Meeting:_____			
8. Was the IEP meeting scheduled at a time that was convenient for you?	☐	☐	☐
9. Was the IEP written at the meeting with input from everybody who was there?	☐	☐	☐
10. Who was at the meeting?			
You	☐	☐	☐
Your spouse	☐	☐	☐
Your child	☐	☐	☐
Your child's teacher	☐	☐	☐
A teacher of the visually handicapped	☐	☐	☐
An orientation and mobility specialist	☐	☐	☐
The director of special education for your school district	☐	☐	☐
The school principal	☐	☐	☐
A member of the evaluation team	☐	☐	☐
Other:_____	☐	☐	☐
Other:_____	☐	☐	☐
Other:_____	☐	☐	☐
11. Does the IEP contain:			
Your child's present level of functioning?	☐	☐	☐
Annual goals?	☐	☐	☐
Short-term objectives?	☐	☐	☐
How the objectives will be measured?	☐	☐	☐
How long it will take to accomplish the objectives?	☐	☐	☐
A statement of the related services your child needs?	☐	☐	☐
Are the related services covered by or reflected in the goals and objectives?	☐	☐	☐
Are the persons responsible for each related service listed?	☐	☐	☐
A statement of the amount of time it is anticipated that your child will be in special education programs?	☐	☐	☐
Does the IEP state when your child will be with nonhandicapped children?	☐	☐	☐
A list of the type of educational aids and devices that your child needs?	☐	☐	☐
12. Did everyone who attended the meeting sign the IEP?	☐	☐	☐

Your Child's Educational Rights, continued

Placement	Yes	No	Not Sure
13. Was your child's placement discussed during the IEP meeting?	☐	☐	☐
14. Does the placement reflect your child's needs?	☐	☐	☐
15. Were you given a choice of placements?	☐	☐	☐
16. Were you told that the ideal placement for your child was not available?	☐	☐	☐
17. Is the class placement located at the same school that your child would attend if he were not visually or multiply handicapped?	☐	☐	☐
18. Does the school building your child is assigned to have:	☐	☐	☐
Braille signs and/or room numbers?	☐	☐	☐
Ramps for wheelchairs?	☐	☐	☐
Bathrooms that are large enough for wheelchairs?	☐	☐	☐
Doors that are wide enough for wheelchairs?	☐	☐	☐
19. Is your child's main teacher trained to work with visually handicapped children?	☐	☐	☐
If not, is a trained teacher of the visually handicapped working with your child as:			
A consultant to the main teacher?	☐	☐	☐
A resource room teacher that your child sees daily?	☐	☐	☐
An itinerant teacher that sees your child daily?	☐	☐	☐
An itinerant teacher that sees your child weekly?	☐	☐	☐
Does your child receive training from an orientation and mobility specialist?	☐	☐	☐

Due Process	Yes	No	Not Sure
20. Were you given a written statement of your due process rights?	☐	☐	☐
Did it tell you what to do if you do not like your child's educational program?	☐	☐	☐
Did it tell you how much time you have in which to do something about your concerns?	☐	☐	☐
Did it tell you whom to call at the school if you are unhappy about your child's educational program?	☐	☐	☐
Did it give you the names of persons or agencies other than the school that might be able to help you?	☐	☐	☐

Turn to page 231 in the HANDBOOK

Chapter 7. LOOKING AHEAD
Choosing a Career

Today's date _____
Your child's
age today _____

Contact your state agency for the blind.

Name _____

Address _____

_____

_____

Telephone _____

What kinds of service are available?

_____

When are they available (how old does your child have to be)?

_____

How do you register for these services?

_____

Ask them to please send any pamphlets or brochures they have about their services.

Contact your state department of vocational rehabilitation.

Name _____

Address _____

_____

_____

Telephone _____

What kinds of service are available?

_____

When are they available (how old does your child have to be)?

_____

How do you register for these services?

_____

Ask them to please send any pamphlets or brochures they have about their services.

← Turn to page 240 in the HANDBOOK

Chapter 7. LOOKING AHEAD
Choosing a Career, continued

Today's date _____
Your child's
age today _____

Contact a local consumers' organization, such as the American Council for the Blind. Ask to visit, if possible, some visually handicapped people on the job. Explain that your child is visually impaired and you would like to know more about working opportunities for your child.

The regional consultant from the American Foundation for the Blind may also be able to direct you to visually or multiply handicapped individuals in the work force. See pages 46–47 of this REACHBOOK for addresses.

Adult's Name: _____

Work Address: _____

_____

_____

Occupation: _____

What modifications does this person make so that he can do his job?

_____

_____

_____

What modifications do other people at the job site make so that this individual can do his job?

_____

_____

_____

Adult's Name: _____

Work Address: _____

_____

_____

Occupation: _____

What modifications does this person make so that he can do his job?

_____

_____

_____

Choosing a Career, continued

What modifications do other people at the job site make so that
this individual can do his job?

_____

_____

_____

Adult's Name: _____

Work Address: _____

_____

_____

Occupation: _____

What modifications does this person make so that he can do his
job?

_____

_____

_____

What modifications do other people at the job site make so that
this individual can do his job?

_____

_____

_____

Adult's Name: _____

Work Address: _____

_____

_____

Occupation: _____

What modifications does this person make so that he can do his
job?

_____

_____

_____

What modifications do other people at the job site make so that this individual can do his job?

_____

_____

_____

Adult's Name: _____

Work Address: _____

_____

_____

Occupation: _____

What modifications does this person make so that he can do his job?

_____

_____

_____

What modifications do other people at the job site make so that this individual can do his job?

_____

_____

_____

Turn to page 242 in the HANDBOOK →

Chapter 7. LOOKING AHEAD
Independent Living

Today's date _____
Your child's
age today _____

Contact a group home facility that accepts visually and/or multiply handicapped adults by checking with Mental Health/Mental Retardation Services. Ask if you could visit one of the residents at work one day. Explain why you want to do so.

Adult's Name: _____

Work Address: _____

_____

_____

Occupation: _____

How does he get to and from work?

_____

_____

What modifications does he need to make to do his job?

_____

_____

_____

What modifications do other people on the job make?

_____

_____

_____

Make contact with visually impaired adults in your community. Ask them about their experiences growing up, and how they decided upon and found their jobs. Keep in mind that times change, so what was relevant years ago may not be relevant now.

Use this page to write down what you found out.

Whom did you call?

Name: _____

Phone: _____

Where did they go to school?

_____

_____

What agencies and organizations were helpful to them?

_____

_____

_____

Is there anything their parents did not do, that they wish they had done?

_____

_____

_____

How did they meet their wives or husbands?

_____

_____

_____

What was the most important thing anyone ever said to them?

_____

_____

_____

Whom did you call?

Name: _____

Phone: _____

Where did they go to school?

_____

What agencies and organizations were helpful to them?

_____

_____

_____

Is there anything their parents did not do, that they wish they had done?

_____

_____

_____

How did they meet their wives or husbands?

_____

_____

_____

Independent Living, continued

What was the most important thing anyone ever said to them?

Turn to page 244 in the HANDBOOK

Chapter 7. LOOKING AHEAD
Parent Support Groups

Attend a parent meeting in your community. If a support group is not available for the visually impaired, join a parents' group for handicapped children.

Name of Group

_____

_____

Telephone number:

_____

Contact person:

_____

Date of meeting you attended:

_____

How did the meeting make you feel?

☐ Happy	☐ Relaxed	☐ Reassured
☐ Depressed	☐ Sad	☐ Lonely
☐ Excited	☐ Frightened	☐ Understood
☐ Misunderstood	☐ Crazy	☐ Supported
☐ Accepted		

Turn to page 246 in the HANDBOOK →

NOTES:

NOTES: